PENGUIN BOOKS — GREAT IDEAS

The Horrors and Absurdities of Religion

Arthur Schopenhauer

1788–1860

Arthur Schopenhauer

The Horrors and Absurdities of Religion

TRANSLATED BY R. J. HOLLINGDALE

PENGUIN BOOKS

Published by the Penguin Group
Penguin Books Ltd, 80 Strand, London WC2R ORL, England
Penguin Group (USA) Inc., 375 Hudson Street, New York, New York 10014, USA
Penguin Group (Canada), 90 Eglinton Avenue East, Suite 700, Toronto, Ontario, Canada M4P 2Y3
(a division of Pearson Penguin Canada Inc.)
Penguin Ireland, 25 St Stephen's Green, Dublin 2, Ireland
(a division of Penguin Books Ltd)
Penguin Group (Australia), 250 Camberwell Road, Camberwell, Victoria 3124, Australia
(a division of Pearson Australia Group Pty Ltd)
Penguin Books India Pvt Ltd, 11 Community Centre, Panchsheel Park, New Delhi – 110 017, India
Penguin Group (NZ), 67 Apollo Drive, Rosedale, North Shore 0632, New Zealand
(a division of Pearson New Zealand Ltd)
Penguin Books (South Africa) (Pty) Ltd, 24 Sturdee Avenue,
Rosebank, Johannesburg 2196, South Africa

Penguin Books Ltd, Registered Offices: 80 Strand, London WC2R ORL, England

www.penguin.com

This translation first published as *Essays and Aphorisms* by Penguin 1970
This selection first published in Penguin Books 2009

004

Translation copyright © R. J. Hollingdale, 1970
All rights reserved

Set by Rowland Phototypesetting Ltd, Bury St Edmunds, Suffolk
Printed in England by Clays Ltd, St Ives plc

978-0-141-19159-1

www.greenpenguin.co.uk

Penguin Books is committed to a sustainable
future for our business, our readers and our planet.
This book is made from Forest Stewardship
Council™ certified paper.

ALWAYS LEARNING   PEARSON

Contents

On Religion: A Dialogue

Demopheles Between ourselves, my dear friend, I don't much like the way you have of displaying your talent for philosophy by making sarcastic remarks about religion or even openly ridiculing it. Every man's faith is sacred to him, therefore it ought to be sacred to you too.

Philalethes Nego consequentiam! [I deny your conclusion!] I can't see why, because other people are simple-minded, I should respect a pack of lies. What I respect is truth, therefore I can't respect what opposes truth. Just as the jurist's motto is: *fiat justitia et pereat mundus* [Let justice be done though the world perish], so my motto is: *vigeat veritas et pereat mundus* [Let truth prosper though the world perish]. Every profession ought to have an analogous device.

Demopheles Then I suppose the physician's would be: *fiant pilulae et pereat mundus* [Let pills be distributed though the world perish] – which would be the one most likely to be realized.

Philalethes Heaven forfend! You must take everything *cum grano salis* [With a pinch of salt].

Demopheles Very well: but that applies to you too: you've got to take religion *cum grano salis*: you've got to see that the needs of ordinary people have to be met in a way they can understand. Religion is the only means of introducing some notion of the high significance of life into the uncultivated heads of the masses, deep sunk as they are in mean pursuits and material drudgery, and of making it palpable to them. Man, taken by and large, has by nature no mind for anything but the satisfaction of his physical needs and desires, and when these are satisfied for a little entertainment and recreation. Philosophers and founders of religions come into the world to shake him out of his stupefaction and to point to the lofty meaning of existence: philosophers for the few, the emancipated, founders of religions for the many, for mankind as a whole. Philosophy isn't for everyone – as your friend Plato said and as you shouldn't forget. Religion is the metaphysics of the people, which they absolutely must be allowed to keep: and that means you have to show an outward respect for it, since to discredit it is to take it away from them. Just as there is folk-poetry and, in the proverbs, folk-wisdom, so there has to be folk-metaphysics: for men have an absolute need for an *interpretation of life*, and it has to be one they are capable of understanding. That is why it is always clothed in allegory; and, as far as its practical effect as a guide to behaviour and its effect on morale as a means of consolation and comfort in suffering and death are concerned, it does as much perhaps as truth itself would do if we possessed it. Don't worry yourself about the baroque and apparently paradoxical forms it assumes: for you, with your learning and culture, have no idea how tortuous and roundabout a route is required to take profound truths to the mass of the people, with their lack of them. The people have no direct access to truth; the various religions are simply schemata by which they grasp it and picture it, but with which it is inseparably linked. Therefore, my dear chap, I hope you'll forgive me for saying that to ridicule them is to be both narrow-minded and unjust.

Philalethes But isn't it just as narrow-minded and unjust to demand that there should exist no other metaphysics except this one cut to the requirements of the people's wants and capacities? that its teachings and doctrine should mark the limit of inquiry and be the guide and model for all thinking, so that the metaphysics of the few and emancipated, as you call them, must amount to nothing but a confirmation, fortification and illumination of your metaphysics of the people? that the highest powers of the human mind should thus lie unused and undeveloped, should indeed be nipped in the bud, in case their activities might happen to run counter to your folk-metaphysics? And do the pretensions of religion amount at bottom to anything less than this? Is it proper and becoming in that which is intolerance and pitilessness itself to preach tolerance and pity? I call on heretic courts and inquisitions, religious wars and crusades, Socrates' poison cup and Bruno's and Vanini's blazing pyres to bear witness! And even if, as I grant, that kind of thing doesn't go on nowadays, what could stand more in the way of genuine philosophy, of honest inquiry after truth, which is the noblest calling of noblest men, than that conventional metaphysics to which the state has granted a monopoly and whose propositions are hammered into everyone's head in his childhood so earnestly and so deeply and firmly that, unless it is of a miraculous degree of elasticity, it retains their impress for ever, so that his capacity for thinking for himself and for making unprejudiced judgements – a capacity which is in any case far from strong – is once and for all paralysed and ruined?

Demopheles What all this really means is that people have acquired a conviction they aren't willing to give up in exchange for yours.

Philalethes If only it *were* a conviction, and one founded on reason! Then it could be combatted with reasons, and we should be fighting on equal terms. But it is common knowledge that religions don't want conviction, on the basis of reasons, but faith, on the basis of revelation. And the capacity for faith is at its strongest in childhood: which is why religions apply themselves before all else to getting these tender years into their possession. It is in this way, even more than by threats and stories of miracles, that the doctrines of faith strike roots: for if, in earliest childhood, a man has certain principles and doctrines repeatedly recited to him with abnormal solemnity and with an air of supreme earnestness such as he has never before beheld, and at the same time the possibility of doubt is never so much as touched on, or if it is only in order to describe it as the first step towards eternal perdition, then the impression produced will be so profound that in almost every case the man will be almost as incapable of doubting this doctrine as of doubting his own existence, so that hardly one in a thousand will then possess the firmness of mind seriously and honestly to ask himself: is this true? The expression *esprits forts*, strong minds, applied to those who do still possess it, is more fitting than those who use it know.

But for the remainder, however, there is nothing so absurd or revolting that they will not firmly believe it once they have been inoculated with it in this fashion. If, for example, the killing of a heretic or an unbeliever were declared to be an essential condition for salvation, then almost every one of them would make doing so one of the main objectives of his life and in death the memory of the deed would provide consolation and strength; as, indeed, almost every Spaniard in fact used to consider an *auto da fé* a most pious and God-pleasing act; to which we have a counterpart in India in the religious fellowship of the Thugs which the English suppressed only quite recently by numerous executions: its members gave proof of their religiousness and of their worship of their goddess Kali by treacherously murdering their friends and travelling companions whenever the occasion offered and making away with their possessions, under the firm illusion that they were doing something praiseworthy and promoting their eternal salvation. The power of religious dogmas imprinted in early years is such that they are capable of stifling conscience and finally all pity and humanity. If you want to see with your own eyes and from close to what early inoculation with faith can do, look at the English. Nature has favoured them before all other nations and furnished them with more understanding, mind, judgement and firmness of character than all the rest; yet they have been degraded lower than all the rest, indeed been rendered almost contemptible, by their stupid church superstition, which infiltrates all their capabilities like an *idée fixe*, a downright monomania. The only reason for this is that education is in the hands of the clergy, who take care so to imprint all the articles of faith in earliest youth that it produces a kind of partial paralysis of the brain, which then gives rise to that lifelong imbecile bigotry through which even people otherwise in the highest degree intelligent degrade themselves and make a quite misleading impression on the rest of the world. But when we consider how essential it is to a masterly performance of this sort that the inoculation with faith should take place during the tenderest years, then the sending of missionaries will no longer seem to us merely the height of importunity, arrogance and impertinence, it will also seem absurd when it is not limited to peoples still in the state of childhood, such as Hottentots, Kaffirs, South Sea Islanders and the like, among whom it has met with the success one would expect; while in India, on the contrary, the Brahmins meet the sermons of missionaries with condescending smiles or a shrug of the shoulders, and among this people in general all attempts at conversion have, the most comfortable opportunity for it notwithstanding, met with utter failure. For, as I have said, childhood and not adulthood is the time to sow the seed of faith, especially when by the time adulthood is reached an earlier seed has already taken root; acquired *conviction*, however, to which adult converts pretend, is as a rule only a mask for some personal interest or other. It is precisely because people feel that this must almost always be the case that a man who changes his religion after reaching years of discretion is everywhere despised by the majority: and this contempt likewise reveals that they regard religion, not as a matter of reasoned conviction, but one of faith inoculated early in life and before having been subjected to any sort of test. That they are justified in their opinion appears from the fact that it is not merely the blindly believing crowd which remains faithful to the religion of its respective fatherland – the priesthood of every religion, which has studied the sources and grounds and dogmas and controversies of this religion, does so too; so that for a priest to cross over from one religion or confession to another is the rarest thing in the world. Thus we see, for example, the Catholic clergy totally convinced of the truth of all the doctrines of its Church, and the Protestant clergy likewise convinced of the truth of all the doctrines of *its* Church, and both defending the doctrines of their confession with equal zeal. Yet this conviction depends entirely on the country in which each was born: to the South German priest the truth of the Catholic dogma is perfectly apparent, but to the North German priest it is that of Protestant dogma which is perfectly apparent. If, then, these convictions, and others like them, rest on objective grounds, these grounds must be climatic; such convictions must be like flowers, the one flourishing only here, the other only there. But the convictions of those who are thus locally convinced are taken on trust everywhere.

Demopheles That does no harm and makes no essential difference; and Protestantism is in fact more suited to the North, Catholicism to the South.

Philalethes It would seem so. But I have adopted a higher viewpoint and I keep a more important objective in sight: advancement of the knowledge of truth in the human race. So far as this is concerned, it is a terrible thing that everyone, wherever he may be born, should have certain assertions impressed on him in earliest youth, together with the assurance that to call them in doubt is to imperil his eternal salvation. I call this a terrible thing because these assertions are largely concerned with what is the basis of all other knowledge we possess, so that a certain point of view in respect to all knowledge is fixed once and for all and, if these assertions should be untrue, it is a permanently perverse point of view; and since, further, their consequences and conclusions extend over our entire system of knowledge, the totality of human understanding is falsified through and through by them. All literature provides evidence of this, that of the Middle Ages most strikingly, but that of the sixteenth and seventeenth centuries still all too well: in all these ages we see even minds of the first rank as if lamed by these false premises, and especially is all insight into the true character and activity of nature shut off to them. Throughout the entire Christian era theism has lain like an incubus on all intellectual, especially philosophical endeavour and has prevented or stunted all progress; and when anyone has possessed the rare elasticity of mind which alone can slip free of these fetters, his writings have been burned and sometimes their author with them, as happened to Bruno and Vanini. – But how completely paralysed *ordinary* minds are by this early metaphysical conditioning can be seen in its most lurid and ludicrous aspect when such a mind ventures to criticize a doctrine different from the one he himself holds. All you find him concerned to do as a rule is to demonstrate that its dogmas differ from those of his own: with that he believes in all simplicity he has proved the falsity of the other doctrine. It really never enters his head to pose the question which of the two might be true: his own articles of faith are to him certain *a priori*.

Demopheles So that is your higher viewpoint. I assure you there is a yet higher one. The saying *Primum vivere, deinde philosophari* [first live, then philosophize] has a more comprehensive meaning than may at first sight appear. – What matters before all else is to restrain the rude and evil dispositions of the mass of the people and so prevent them from perpetrating acts of violence, cruelty and infamy and the more extreme forms of injustice: and if you delayed doing that until they had come to recognize and understand truth, you would infallibly have to wait for ever. For even supposing truth had already been discovered, they would be incapable of grasping it: they would still need to have it clothed in allegory, parable, myth. As Kant has said, there must always be a public standard of right and virtue, and this standard must indeed always be seen fluttering high in the breeze. In the last resort it is a matter of indifference which heraldic figure stands upon it, provided only it correctly indicates what is meant. Such an allegorical representation of truth is for mankind as a whole everywhere and always an answerable substitute for the truth itself, which is for ever inaccessible to it, and for philosophy in general, which it will never comprehend – quite apart from the fact that this changes every day and has never yet assumed a form which has won universal recognition. So you see, my dear Philalethes, practical aims take precedence over theoretical ones in every respect.

Philalethes This whole point of view is as misguided as it is nowadays universally praised and popular: which is why I now hasten to enter a protest against it. It is *untrue* that state, law and justice can be maintained only with the assistance of religion and its articles, and that the judiciary and the police require it as their necessary complement for preserving public order. It is *untrue*, though it were reiterated a hundred times. For the ancients, and especially the Greeks, provide us with a factual and striking *instantia in contrarium*: they possessed nothing whatever of what we understand by *religion*. They had no sacred scriptures, and they had no dogmas which were taught, adherence to which was demanded of everybody, and which were imprinted on the minds of children. Nor did the administrators of their religion preach morals or worry about what people were doing or not doing. Absolutely not! The duties of the priests extended no further than temple ceremonial, prayers, hymns, sacrifices, processions, lustrations, and so forth, all of which has nothing to do with the moral improvement of the individual. The whole of so-called religion consisted rather in seeing that this or that god was provided with a temple in which his cult was carried on under the offices of the state, which cult was therefore at bottom a police matter. No man, apart from the functionaries involved, was in any way obliged to attend these ceremonies, or even to believe in the cult. No trace of a duty to believe in any dogma whatever is to be discovered in the whole of antiquity. Only if a man publicly denied the existence of the gods, or otherwise disparaged them, did he render himself liable to punishment: for then he affronted the state, which served them: but apart from this everyone was free to decide for himself how much he believed. Of the immortality of the soul and a life after death the ancients, far from having a dogmatically fixed conception, had no firm or clear conception at all; their ideas on these subjects were altogether loose, vacillating, indefinite and problematic, and each had his own; and their ideas about their gods were equally various, individual and vague. Thus the ancients really had no *religion* in our sense of the word. But did anarchy and lawlessness reign among them because they had no religion? did they not rather produce law and civic order to such purpose that it still remains as the basis of our own? was property not completely secure, even though it consisted in a large degree of slaves? And did this state of things not endure for well over a thousand years? – So I cannot acknowledge that religion has a practical objective, nor that it is indispensably necessary as the basis of all civil order. For if such were the case, then the sacred endeavour to attain to light and truth would appear at the least quixotic, and if it should venture to denounce the official faith as a usurper who had taken over the throne of truth and maintained its seat by perpetual deception, it would appear criminal.

Demopheles But religion is not antithetical to truth; for it itself teaches truth; only, because its field of action is not a narrow lecture-room but the whole world and all mankind, it has to adapt itself to the needs and abilities of a large and assorted public, and cannot present the truth naked. Religion is truth expressed in allegory and myth and thus made accessible and digestible to mankind at large: for mankind at large could never endure it pure and unalloyed, just as we cannot live on pure oxygen. The profound meaning and lofty goal of life can be revealed to the people and kept before their eyes only in *symbolical* form, because the people are not capable of grasping it literally. Philosophy, on the other hand, should, like the Eleusinian Mysteries, be reserved for the few and select.

Philalethes I understand: what it comes down to is that truth is to be clothed in lies. But that is an alliance which will ruin it: for what a dangerous weapon you place in a man's hands when you grant him the right to employ untruth as a vehicle for truth! If that is allowed, then I fear untruth will do more harm than the truth it carries will ever do good. If allegory would confess itself to be such then indeed I might not object: only, if it did that, it would forfeit all respect and consequently all effectiveness. It therefore has to put itself forward as true *sensu proprio*, whereas it is at the most true *sensu allegorico*. Here lies the incurable harm, the enduring evil which has always brought religion into conflict with the noble, unprejudiced endeavour to attain to pure truth, and which will always do so.

Demopheles Not at all: that too has been guarded against. For though religion may not openly confess its allegorical nature, it nonetheless gives sufficient indication of it.

Philalethes How does it do that?

Demopheles Through its mysteries. 'Mystery' is even at bottom the theological *terminus technicus* for religious allegory. All religions, moreover, have their mysteries. Properly speaking, a mystery is an obviously absurd dogma which nonetheless conceals a lofty truth in itself completely incomprehensible to the common understanding of the uncultivated mass of the people, who then absorb this truth thus disguised and take it on trust without being misled by the absurdity which is obvious to them too: thus they participate in the kernel of the matter in so far as it is possible for them to do so. You will understand better what I mean when I say that mystery is employed in philosophy too, as when, for example, Pascal, who was pietist, mathematician and philosopher in one, says in this threefold capacity: God is everywhere centre and nowhere periphery. Malebranche too has rightly said: *La liberté est un mystère.* – One could go further and assert that everything in religions is really mystery: for to impart truth *sensu proprio* to the people in its uncultivated state is absolutely impossible: all it is capable of is enlightenment through an allegorical reflexion of it. Naked truth does not belong before the eyes of the profane vulgar: it must appear before them heavily veiled. Hence it is quite unreasonable to require of a religion that it shall be true *sensu proprio*. Myth and allegory are its proper element: but under this unavoidable condition, imposed by the mental limitations of the great multitude, it offers sufficient satisfaction to the ineradicable metaphysical need of man, and takes the place of pure philosophical truth, which is infinitely difficult to attain and perhaps never will be attained.

Philalethes Oh yes, more or less as a wooden leg takes the place of a natural one: it substitutes for it, does duty for it as best it can, claims to be regarded as a natural leg, is artificially put together well or less well, and so on. The only difference is that, while a natural leg as a rule preceded the wooden one, religion has everywhere got the start on philosophy.

Demopheles That may be: but if you haven't got a natural leg a wooden one is very useful. You must bear in mind that the metaphysical need of man absolutely demands satisfaction, because the horizon of his thoughts must be closed and not remain unbounded. But man has as a rule no capacity for weighing reasons and then deciding between true and false; moreover, the labour which nature and its needs impose upon him leaves him no time for such inquiries, nor for the education they presuppose. In his case, therefore, there can be no question of conviction by reasons: he must be referred to belief and authority. Even if a really true philosophy had taken the place of religion, nine-tenths of mankind at the very least would receive it on authority, so that it too would be a matter of belief. Authority, however, can be established only by time and circumstance: it cannot be bestowed upon that which has only reasons in its favour. It must be allowed to that which has acquired it during the course of history, even if it is only an allegorical representation of truth. This representation, supported by authority, appeals first of all to the actual metaphysical predisposition of man, to the theoretical need which arises from the importunate enigma of our existence and from the consciousness that behind the world's physical plane there must be concealed a metaphysical, something unchanging which serves as a basis for the world's continual change; then, however, it appeals to the will, to the fears and hopes of mortals living in constant distress, for whom it accordingly creates gods and demons on whom they can call, whom they can appease, whom they can win over; finally, it appeals to the moral consciousness undeniably present in man, to which it lends external stay and confirmation, a support without which it would not easily be able to maintain itself in the struggle with so many temptations. It is precisely from this side that religion affords an inexhaustible source of consolation and comfort in the countless and great sufferings of life which does not desert men even in the hour of death but rather only then reveals its full efficacy. Religion may thus be compared to one who takes a blind man by the hand and leads him, since he cannot see for himself and the sole point is that he should arrive at his destination, not that he should see all there is to see.

Philalethes This last aspect is certainly the strong point of religion. If it is a *fraus*, it is a *pia fraus* [pious fraud]: that is undeniable. But this makes a priest into a curious cross between a deceiver and a moralist. For they durst not teach the real truth, as you have quite rightly explained, even if they knew it, which they do not. So that a true philosophy is possible, but not a true religion: I mean true in the proper meaning of the word, and not merely metaphorically or allegorically true in the way you have described; in that sense all religions would be true, only in differing degrees. In any event, it is quite in keeping with the inextricable tangle of weal and woe, honesty and deceit, goodness and badness, nobility and baseness which the world as a rule presents us with that the weightiest, loftiest and most sacred truth can make its appearance only when adulterated with a lie, has indeed to borrow strength from a lie as from something which makes a stronger impression on mankind, and must be ushered in by a lie in the form of revelation. One could even regard this fact as the distinguishing mark of the moral world. However, let us not abandon the hope that mankind will one day reach the point of maturity and education at which it is capable of on the one hand producing and on the other receiving true philosophy. *Simplex sigillum veri* [simplicity is the seal of truth]: naked truth must be so simple and intelligible that it can be imparted to everyone in its true shape without adulterating it with myths and fables (a mass of lies) – that is, without disguising it as *religion*.

Demopheles You have an inadequate idea of how limited the capacity of most people is.

Philalethes It was merely a hope I was expressing: but it is a hope which I cannot give up. If it were fulfilled it would of course drive religion from the place which it has so long occupied in its stead but by that very means kept open for it. Religion would have fulfilled its task and run its course: it could then release the race it has conducted to its majority and itself pass peacefully away. This would be the euthanasia of religion. But as long as it lives it has two faces: one the face of truth, the other the face of deception. You will love it or detest it according to whether you keep one or the other face in view. You have to regard it as a necessary evil, its necessity deriving from the wretched imbecility of the majority of mankind, which is incapable of understanding truth and therefore, in this pressing case, requires a substitute for it.

Demopheles Hold to that conclusion, then, and bear always in mind that religion has two sides. If it cannot be justified from the theoretical, that is to say intellectual side, from the moral side it proves to be the sole means of guiding, controlling and appeasing this race of animals endowed with reason whose kinship with the ape does not exclude kinship with the tiger. If you consider religion in this light and remember that its aims are above all practical and only secondarily theoretical, it will appear to you as worthy of the highest respect.

Philalethes Which respect would rest ultimately on the principle that the end sanctifies the means. I have no inclination for a compromise founded on that basis. Religion may be an excellent means of taming and training the perverse, obtuse and wicked biped race: but in the eyes of the friend of truth every fraud, however pious, is still a fraud. A pack of lies would be a strange means of inducing virtue. The flag to which I have sworn allegiance is truth: I shall stay faithful to it everywhere and, regardless of the outcome, fight for light and truth. If I see the religions in the ranks of the enemy . . .

Demopheles But you won't find them there! Religion is no deception: it is true and is the most important of all truths. But because, as I have already said, its doctrines are of so lofty a kind that the multitude could not grasp them directly; because, I say, its light would blind the common eye; it appears veiled in allegory and teaches that which, while not strictly true in itself, is true in respect of the lofty meaning contained within it: and thus understood, religion is truth.

Philalethes That would be fair enough – if it could only venture to present itself as true in a merely allegorical sense. But it comes forward claiming to be true in the strict and proper sense of the word: therein lies the deception, and here is the point at which the friend of truth must oppose it.

Demopheles But that is *conditio sine qua non* [indispensable condition]. If religion were to admit that it was only the allegorical meaning of its doctrine which was true this would rob it of all efficacy; through such rigorousness its incalculably beneficial influence on the heart and morality of men would be lost. You ought to guard against letting your theoretical cavilling discredit in the eyes of the people and finally wrest from them something which is an inexhaustible source of consolation and comfort, and which they need so much, indeed with their hard lot need more than we do: for this reason alone it ought to be inviolable.

Philalethes With *that* argument you could have driven Luther from the field when he attacked the sale of indulgences. – Truth, my friend, truth alone holds firm, endures and stays steadfast: truth's consolation is the only solid consolation: it is the indestructible diamond.

Demopheles Yes, if you had truth in your pocket, and could favour us with it on demand. But all you have is metaphysical systems about which nothing is certain but the head-cudgelling they cost. Before you deprive someone of something you must have something better to put in its place.

Philalethes Oh, to have to go on hearing that said! To free a man from an error is not to deprive him of anything but to give him something: for the knowledge that a thing is false is a piece of truth. No error is harmless: sooner or later it will bring misfortune to him who harbours it. Therefore deceive no one, but rather confess ignorance of what you do not know, and leave each man to devise his own articles of faith for himself.

Demopheles A particularism of that sort is totally opposed to human nature and would consequently be the end of all social order. Man is an *animal metaphysicum*, that is, his metaphysical need is more urgent than any other; he thus conceives life above all according to its metaphysical meaning and wants to see everything in the light of that. Consequently, and however strange it may sound in view of the uncertainty of all dogma, agreement on fundamental metaphysical views is the chief thing for man, because genuine and lasting social union is possible only among those who do agree on these. The social structure, the state, will stand quite firm only when it is founded on a universally recognized metaphysical system. Such a system can naturally be only one of folk-metaphysics, that is, religion; which is then fused with the state constitution and with every social manifestation of the people's life, as it also is with every solemn act of private life. The social structure could hardly exist at all if religion did not lend weight to the government's authority and the ruler's dignity.

Philalethes Oh yes, princes use the Lord God as a bogy to get their grown-up children to bed when nothing else will any longer serve; which is why they value him so highly. Very well; but I would advise every ruler to sit down every half-year on a certain fixed date and carefully read the fifteenth chapter of the First Book of Samuel, so as always to have in mind what it means to use the altar to support the throne. Moreover, since that *ultima ratio theologorum* [final argument of theology], the stake, has gone out of use the effectiveness of this means of government has much diminished. For, as you know, religions are like glow-worms: they need darkness in order to shine. A certain degree of general ignorance is the condition for the existence of any religion, the element in which alone it is able to live. Perhaps the day so often prophesied will soon come when religions will depart from European man like a nurse whose care the child has outgrown and which henceforth comes under the instruction of a tutor. For articles of faith based on nothing but authority, miracles and revelation are beyond doubt short-term aids appropriate only to the childhood of mankind: and it must be admitted that a race which, according to all the indications provided by physical and historical data, is at present no older than one hundred times the life of a man of sixty, is still in its first childhood.

Demopheles Oh if, instead of prophesying with uncon-cealed delight the end of Christianity, you would only consider how infinitely great a debt European man owes to it! He received from Christianity an outlook pre-viously unfamiliar to him, an outlook deriving from knowledge of the fundamental truth that life cannot be an end in itself, but that the true end of our existence lies beyond life. For the Greeks and Romans had placed it entirely *within* life, in which respect at any rate they can be called blind heathen. All their virtues consequently can be traced back to qualities serviceable to the community, to useful qualities, and Aristotle says naïvely: 'Those virtues must necessarily be the greatest which are the most useful to others.' Christianity liberated European man from this exclusive involvement in an ephemeral and uncertain existence. The Greeks and Romans had forgotten the serious, true and profound significance of life: they lived heedlessly, like grown-up children, until Christianity came and called them back to life's earnestness.

Philalethes And to judge how it succeeded we have only to compare antiquity with the Middle Ages which followed it, the age of Pericles, say, with the fourteenth century. You would hardly think you were dealing with the same species. In the former the fairest unfolding of humanity, a splendid state structure, wise laws, a carefully balanced legal administration, rationally regulated freedom, all the arts, together with poetry and philosophy, at their peak, creating works which after thousands of years still stand as unequalled models of their kind, almost as the productions of higher beings whom we can never hope to emulate, and at the same time life beautified by the noblest social fellowship such as we see reflected in *The Symposium* of Xenophon. And now look at the latter age, if you are able to. Look at the age when the Church had fettered the minds and forced the bodies of mankind, so that knights and priests might lay all the drudgery of life on their common beasts of burden, the third estate. Here you find *force majeure*, feudalism and fanaticism in intimate alliance, and in their train hideous ignorance and darkness of mind, and in consequence intolerance, quarrelling over beliefs, religious wars, crusades, persecution of heretics and inquisitions; while social fellowship took the form of a knightly chivalry compounded of brutality and foppishness, with grotesqueries and humbug pedantically reduced to a system, with degrading superstition and apish veneration of women. The ancients were unquestionably less cruel than the Middle Ages; and they were, moreover, very tolerant, laid great stress on justice, frequently sacrificed themselves for their country, and displayed such nobility of every kind and so genuine a humanity that to this very day an acquaintanceship with their thoughts and actions is called a study of the humanities. Their tolerance of pederasty, which is certainly reprehensible and the principal reproach now made against the morality of the ancients, is a trifling thing compared with the Christian abominations I have mentioned, and that this practice is less evident now by no means implies that it is that much less prevalent. All things considered, can you maintain that mankind has really been made morally better by Christianity?

Demopheles If the results have not everywhere corresponded to the purity and truth of the doctrine it may be because this doctrine has been too noble, too exalted for mankind, and its goal has therefore been placed too high: it was certainly easier to comply with heathen morality, as it is with Mohammedan. What is most exalted is always most open to abuse and imposture; so that these lofty doctrines too have sometimes served as a pretext for the most atrocious proceedings and acts of wickedness.

Philalethes It would really be an extremely useful inquiry to try to make a completely impartial and accurate assessment of the advantages derived from religion compared with the disadvantages which have attended it. But that would require a much greater quantity of historical and psychological data than we two have at our command. Academies could make it the subject of a prize essay.

Demopheles They will take care not to do so.

Philalethes I am surprised you should say that: for it is a bad sign for religion. – If only a statistician could tell us first of all how many crimes are refrained from each year from religious motives and how many from other motives. There would be very few of the former. For when a man feels tempted to commit a crime, then you can depend on it that the first thing he thinks of in opposition to the idea is the punishment appointed for it and the probability of its falling upon him; the second consideration is the risk to his honour. On these two objections he will, if I am not mistaken, ponder for hours before religious considerations so much as occur to him. If, however, he gets over these two first bulwarks against crime, I believe that religion *alone* will very rarely hold him back.

Demopheles But I believe it will do so very often, especially when its influence is already operative through the medium of custom, so that a man immediately shrinks from committing any great act of wickedness. Early impressions are enduring.

Philalethes Suppose a public proclamation were suddenly made at this moment repealing all laws relating to crime: I fancy neither you nor I would have the courage even to go home alone under the protection of religious motives. If, on the other hand, all religions were in the same way declared untrue, we should go on living as before under the protection of the law alone without any special precautions. – But I will go further, and say that religions have very frequently had a decidedly harmful influence on morality. It may be asserted as a generalization that what is given to God is taken from men, inasmuch as it is very easy to substitute adulation of the former for decent behaviour towards the latter. In every religion, faith, temple ceremonies and rites of all kinds soon come to be pronounced of more immediate interest to the divine will than moral actions; indeed, the former, especially when they are bound up with the emoluments of the priests, gradually come to be regarded as a substitute for the latter: animal sacrifices, or the saying of masses, or the founding of chapels, or the erection of wayside crosses, soon come to be the most meritorious works, so that they atone for even the gravest crimes, as do penances, subjection to priestly authority, confessions, pilgrimages, donations to the temples and their priests, the building of monasteries, and the like, whereby the priests finally appear as virtually no more than go-betweens in a trade with bribable gods. And even if it doesn't go as far as that, where is the religion whose adherents do not consider at any rate prayers, hymns and various acts of devotion as at least a partial substitute for moral conduct? – But to return to the main point: you are certainly right to urge the strong metaphysical need of mankind, but religion appears to me not so much the satisfaction as the abuse of this need. We have seen that at any rate as regards the advancement of morality its utility is in great part problematic, while its disadvantages and especially the atrocities which have followed in its train are patently obvious. The matter bears another complexion, to be sure, if we consider the utility of religion as a prop for thrones, for where these are held by the grace of God altar and throne stand in the closest association: every wise prince who loves his throne and his family will consequently always set himself up before his people as a model of true religiousness.

Demopheles Well, after all the trouble I have taken I am sorry not to have altered your attitude towards religion: on the other hand, I can assure you that nothing *you* have adduced has succeeded in shaking my conviction of its high value and necessity.

Philalethes I believe you: for, as it says in *Hudibras*:

> A man convinced against his will
> Is of the same opinion still.

But I console myself with the thought that, with controversies and mineral baths alike, the only real effect is the after-effect.

Demopheles Then let me wish you a pleasant after-effect.

Philalethes You might have your wish if only my stomach could digest a certain Spanish proverb.

Demopheles Which is?

Philalethes *Detras de la cruz está el Diablo.*

Demopheles Which is in English?

Philalethes Behind the Cross stands the Devil.

Demopheles Come, don't let us part with sarcasms. Let us see rather that, like Janus – or better, like Yama, the Brahmin god of death – religion has two faces, one very friendly, one very gloomy: you have had your eyes fixed on one face, I have had mine fixed on the other.

Philalethes You are right, old man!

On Ethics

1

That the world has no ethical significance but only a physical one is the greatest and most pernicious of errors, the fundamental error, the intrinsically *perverse* view, and is probably at bottom also that which faith has personified as the Anti-Christ. Nevertheless, and despite all the religions, which all assert the opposite and seek to demonstrate it in mythical form, this fundamental error never quite dies out on earth but raises its head again and again until general indignation again and again compels it to hide it.

As a consequence of their profounder ethical and meta-physical insight, the *Buddhists* start not with cardinal virtues but with cardinal vices, as the antitheses or negations of which the cardinal virtues first appear. According to J. J. Schmidt's *Geschichte der Ostmongolen* the Buddhist cardinal vices are lust, sloth, wrath and avarice, although pride should probably stand in place of sloth, as it does in the *Lettres édifiantes et curieuses* (edition of 1819), where, however, envy or hatred is added as a fifth. The sufis too lay down the same cardinal vices, arranged very strikingly in couples, so that lust is paired with avarice and wrath with pride. We find lust, wrath and avarice already laid down as cardinal vices in the *Bhagavad Gita*, which is evidence of the extreme antiquity of the doctrine. These three cardinal vices likewise appear in the *Prabodha-Chandrodaya*, an allegorical philosophical drama very important for the Vedanta, where they are the three commanders in the service of King Passion in his war against King Reason. It would follow that the cardinal virtues antithetical to these cardinal vices are chastity and generosity, together with gentleness and humility.

If you now compare with these profound basic concepts of oriental ethics the celebrated and thousand-times reiterated Platonic cardinal virtues, justice, bravery, moderation, and wisdom, you will find the latter do not derive from any clear, guiding basic concept and are therefore superficial and in part, even, obviously false. Virtues are qualities of will: wisdom belongs first and foremost to the intellect. *Sophrosune*, which Cicero translates as *temperantia* and which is in German *Mässigkeit* and in English *moderation*, is a very vague and ambiguous expression under which many different things can be subsumed, such as prudence, sobriety, keeping one's head. Bravery is not a virtue at all: though it is sometimes a servant or instrument of virtue, it is just as ready to serve the unworthiest ends: actually it is a temperamental quality. Even so early a writer as Geulinx rejects the Platonic cardinal virtues (in his *Ethics*) and substitutes *diligentia, obedientia, justitia, humilitas* – an obviously bad selection. The Chinese name five cardinal virtues: pity, justice, politeness, wisdom and honesty (*Journal asiatique*, vol. 9) – Christianity has not cardinal but theological virtues: faith, hope and charity.

What distinguishes a moral virtue from a moral vice is whether the basic feeling towards others behind it is one of envy or one of pity: for every man bears these two diametrically opposed qualities within him, inasmuch as they arise from the comparison between his own condition and that of others which he cannot help making; one or other of these qualities will become his basic disposition and determine the nature of his actions according to the effect this comparison has on his individual character. Envy reinforces the wall between Thou and I: pity makes it thin and transparent; indeed, it sometimes tears the wall down altogether, whereupon the distinction between I and Not-I disappears.

3

That *bravery* which was spoken of above – or more precisely *courage*, which is what lies behind it (for bravery is only courage in war) – deserves to be looked at more closely. The ancients included courage among the virtues, cowardice among the vices: this assessment does not accord with the Christian outlook, which is directed towards sufferance and benevolence and whose doctrine forbids all enmity and, properly speaking, even resistance; so that this assessment of courage and cowardice no longer obtains. We have nonetheless to admit that cowardice does not seem to us to be very consistent with a noble character, the reason being that it betrays a too great solicitude for one's own person. Courage however implies that one is willing to face a present evil so as to prevent a greater evil in the future, while cowardice does the reverse. Now the nature of *endurance* is similar to that ascribed to courage, for endurance consists precisely in the clear consciousness that there exist greater evils than those present at the moment but that in seeking to escape or prevent the latter one might call down the former. Courage would consequently be a kind of *endurance*; and, since it is endurance which gives us the capacity for self-denial and self-overcoming of any kind, courage too is, through it, at any rate related to virtue.

Yet the question can perhaps be considered from an even higher point of view. It might be possible to trace all fear of death back to a deficiency in that natural metaphysic by virtue of which man bears within him the certainty that he exists just as much in everyone else, indeed in everything else, as he does in his own person, whose death cannot therefore be of very much concern to him. Possession of this certainty would, on the other hand, be the origin of heroic courage, which would consequently have the same origin as the virtues of justice and philanthropy. This is, to be sure, to look at the matter from a very exalted standpoint: on the other hand, it is not otherwise easy to explain why cowardice should be considered contemptible, personal courage noble and sublime; since from any lower standpoint there seems to be no reason why a finite individual which is to itself all-in-all – is indeed itself the fundamental condition for the existence of the rest of the world – should not place the preservation of this self before all else. A wholly immanent, that is to say purely empirical, explanation based on the utility of courage would be inadequate.

4

Every good human quality is related to a bad one into which it threatens to pass over; and every bad quality is similarly related to a good one. The reason we so often misunderstand people is that when we first make their acquaintance we mistake their bad qualities for the related good ones, or vice versa: thus a prudent man will seem cowardly, a thrifty one avaricious; or a spendthrift will seem liberal, a boor frank and straightforward, an impudent fellow full of noble self-confidence, and so on.

5

Whoever lives among men will again and again be tempted to assume that moral wickedness and intellectual incapacity are closely connected and spring from one root. The impression that this is so arises merely because they are so often found together; and this can be explained by the very frequent occurrence of both, which means they often have to live together under the same roof. Not that it can be denied that they play into the hands of one another to their mutual advantage,

which is why so many people present so very disagreeable an appearance and why the world is as it is. For
want of understanding is favourable for making baseness,
wickedness and falsity appear visibly, while cleverness
knows better how to conceal them. And, on the other
hand, how often perversity prevents a man from seeing
truths that his reason is quite capable of grasping.

Yet let no one give himself airs. Just as everyone, even
the greatest genius, is decidedly stupid and ignorant in
some sphere or other of knowledge and thereby pro-
claims his kinship with the essentially perverse and
absurd human race, so everyone bears within him something altogether morally bad, and even the finest, indeed
noblest character will sometimes surprise us by revealing
distinct traits of baseness, as though he was thereby
seeking to own his kinship with the human race, in
which every degree of vileness is to be discovered.

With all this, however, the difference between man
and man is incalculably great, and many would be
appalled if they could see others as they really are. – Oh
for an Asmodeus of morals who would let his minions
see not only through roofs and walls but also through
the veil of pretence, falsity, hypocrisy, lies and deception
which extends over everything, so that they would know
how little true honesty there is in the world and how
often, even where one least suspects it, all the virtuous
outworks merely conceal the fact that, secretly and in
the innermost recess, dishonesty sits at the helm. For
our civilized world is nothing but a great masquerade.
You encounter knights, parsons, soldiers, doctors,
lawyers, priests, philosophers and a thousand more: but

they are not what they appear – they are merely masks behind which as a rule money-grubbers are hiding. One man puts on the mask of justice the better to attack his fellows; another, with the same object in view, chooses that of public good and patriotism; a third that of religion and purity of faith. Many have put on the mask of philosophy, philanthropy and the like for their various ends. Women have a narrower range to choose from: usually they employ the masks of modesty, coyness, simplicity and demureness. Then there are universal masks without any special character, as it were domi-noes, which are therefore to be met with everywhere: among these are strict honesty, politeness, sincere sympathy and grinning affability. Usually, as I say, there is nothing but industrialists, businessmen and speculators concealed behind all these masks. In this respect the only honest class is that of the tradesmen, since they alone give themselves out for what they are: they go about without any mask on, and thus they stand low in the social order.

But there are more serious considerations involved and worse things to report. Man is at bottom a dreadful wild animal. We know this wild animal only in the tamed state called civilization and we are therefore shocked by occasional outbreaks of its true nature: but if and when the bolts and bars of the legal order once fall apart and anarchy supervenes it reveals itself for what it is. For enlightenment on this matter, though, you have no need to wait until that happens: there exist hundreds of reports, recent and less recent, which will suffice to convince you that man is in no way inferior to the tiger or the hyena in pitilessness and cruelty. A weighty contemporary example is provided by the reply received by the British Anti-Slavery Society from the American Anti-Slavery Society in answer to its inquiries about the treatment of slaves in the slave-owning states of the North American Union: *Slavery and the Internal Slave-Trade in the United States of North America*. This book constitutes one of the heaviest of all indictments against mankind. No one can read it without horror, and few will not be reduced to tears: for whatever the reader of it may have heard or imagined or dreamed of the unhappy condition of the slaves, indeed of human harshness and cruelty in general, will fade into insignificance when he reads how these devils in human form, these bigoted, church-going, Sabbath-keeping scoundrels, especially the Anglican parsons among them, treat their innocent black brothers whom force and injustice have delivered into their devilish clutches. This book, which consists of dry but authentic and documented reports, rouses one's human feelings to such a degree of indignation that one could preach a crusade for the subjugation and punishment of the slave-owning states of North America. They are a blot on mankind. – But we do not need to go to the New World for examples. In the year 1848 it came to light that in England a husband or wife, or both in collusion, had not *once* but a hundred times poisoned their children one after the other, or tortured them to death with hunger and neglect, merely for the insurance money from burial clubs; children were insured with several, in some cases as many as twenty, such clubs (see *The Times*, 20, 22 and 23 September 1848).

Reports of this sort belong, it is true, to the blackest pages of mankind's criminal record. But the source of them and of everything like them is the inner and inborn nature of man, in which the first and foremost quality is a colossal egoism ready and eager to overstep the bounds of justice. Does the admitted necessity for a so anxiously guarded European balance of power not already contain a confession that man is a beast of prey which will pounce upon a weaker neighbour as soon as he notices his existence? And is this fact not confirmed every day in ordinary life?

Gobineau (*Des races humaines*) called man *l'animal méchant par excellence*, which people took very ill because they felt it was aimed at them. But Gobineau was right: for man is the only animal which causes pain to others with no other object than causing pain. The other animals do it in the cause of appeasing their hunger or in the rage of battle. No animal ever torments another for the sake of tormenting: but man does so, and it is this which constitutes the *diabolical* nature which is far worse than the merely bestial.

The worst trait in human nature, however, is *Schadenfreude*, since it is closely related to cruelty, indeed differs from this only as theory differs from practice, but generally arises under circumstances in which pity ought to arise, which, as its antithesis, is the true source of all genuine justice and love of mankind. The antithesis of pity in another sense is *envy*, inasmuch as it is excited by an antithetical cause: that it is the antithesis of pity derives first and foremost from what causes it, and only as a consequence of this cause does it become the feeling of envy itself. Thus envy, although reprehensible, admits of some excuse and is humanly understandable, while *Schadenfreude* is diabolical and its derision is the laughter of Hell.

Now if, having taken stock of human *wickedness* as we have just done, you feel a sense of horror at it, you should straightaway turn your eyes to the *misery* of human existence. (And if you are shocked at its misery you should turn your eyes to its wickedness.) Then you will see that they balance one another; you will become aware of the existence of an eternal justice, that the world itself is its own universal Last Judgement, and you will begin to understand why everything that lives must atone for its existence, first by living and then by dying.

6

Readers of my ethical philosophy will know that with me the foundation of morality ultimately rests on the truth which is in the Veda and Vedanta expressed in the mystical formula *tat twam asi* (This art Thou), by which is meant every living thing, whether man or animal: it is called the *Mahavakya*, the great word.

The recognition of one's own essential being in another, objectively present individual is most clearly and beautifully evident in those cases in which a human being already on the brink of death is anxiously and actively concerned with the welfare and rescue of others. Of this kind is the well-known story of the servant girl who was one night bitten in the yard by a mad dog; believing herself beyond help, she seized the dog, dragged it to the kennel and locked the door, so that no one else should fall victim to it. Another example is the incident in Naples immortalized by Tischbein in one of his water colours: a son bearing his aged father on his back is fleeing from a stream of lava which is rushing down towards the sea; when there remains only a narrow strip of land left between the two destructive elements, the father bids his son lay him down and save himself, since otherwise both will perish. The son obeys and in departing looks back at his father in a last farewell. This is what the painting depicts. Entirely apposite too is the historical event depicted by the masterly hand of Walter Scott in *The Heart of Midlothian*: two criminals have been condemned to death; one of them, whose ineptitude has led to the capture of the other, overpowers the guard in the church after the funeral sermon and succeeds in freeing his companion without making any attempt to free himself. Also to be included here indeed – although the Western reader might find it offensive – is a scene often reproduced in copperplate print in which a soldier kneeling to be shot by a firing-squad is violently shooing away his dog, who is running up to him. – In every case of this kind we see an individual who is with perfect certainty going to meet his immediate destruction ceasing to think about his own preservation in order to direct all his attention and effort to that of another. What could possibly express more clearly the consciousness that this destruction is only the destruction of a phenomenon and is therefore itself phenomenon, while the essential being of him who faces destruction remains unaffected: it continues to exist in the other in whom at precisely this point he so clearly recognizes it, as his actions prove. For if this were not so; if we had before us a being actually about to be annihilated; how could this being betray so intense an interest in the welfare and continued existence of another as it does betray in expending its last energies to this end?

There are in fact two antithetical ways of becoming conscious of one's own existence: firstly, by empirical perception, by seeing it as it appears from without, an evanescently small existence in a world boundless in space and time, as one among the thousand million human beings who run around on this earth and do so for a very brief time, renewing themselves every thirty years; secondly, however, by plunging into one's own inner self and realizing that it is all-in-all and actually the only real being which, as an addition, sees itself reflected in its outward form as if in a mirror. That the former mode of knowledge comprehends merely phenomena conveyed through the agency of the *principium individuationis*, but the latter is a direct perception of one's being as thing in itself – this is a theory in which I am supported as regards the first part by Kant, but as regards both parts by the Veda. The simple objection to the latter mode of knowledge is, of course, that it presupposes that one and the same being can be at different places at the same time and yet be wholly present in each of them. But if this is from the empirical standpoint a palpable impossibility, indeed an absurdity, it is nonetheless perfectly true of the thing in itself, because that impossibility and absurdity depends entirely on the phenomenal forms which constitute the *principium individuationis*. For the thing in itself, the will to live, is present whole and undivided in every single being, even the most insignificant, as completely as in all that have ever been, are or will be, taken together. And in truth, if every other being were to perish, the entire being in itself of the world would still exist unharmed and undiminished in this single one remaining and would laugh at the destruction of all the rest as an illusion. This is, to be sure, a conclusion *per impossibile*, to which one is quite entitled to oppose this other, that if any being whatever, even the most insignificant, were to be utterly annihilated, the whole world would perish in and with it. It is in precisely this sense that the mystic Angelus Silesius says:

> Ich weiss, dass ohne mich Gott nicht ein Nu kann leben:
> Werd' ich zunicht; er muss von Noth den Geist aufgeben.
> [I know that without me God cannot live for an instant:
> If I perish he must needs give up the ghost.]

7

After my prize essay on moral freedom no thinking person can remain in any doubt that moral freedom is never to be sought in nature but only outside of nature. It is metaphysical; in the physical world it is impossible. Our individual actions are, consequently, in no way free;

on the other hand, the individual character of each of us must be regarded as a free act. It is as it is because it wants, once and for all, to be as it is. For will itself and in itself – even when it appears as an individual and thus constitutes the individual's original and fundamental volition – is independent of all knowledge, because it precedes all knowledge. What it receives from knowledge is merely the motivations by which its nature evolves in successive stages and makes itself distinguishable or visible: but will itself, since it lies outside of time, is unchangeable for as long as it exists at all. So that every individual, as he once and for all is, and under the circumstances obtaining at any particular moment – which for their part are governed by strict necessity – can absolutely never do anything other than precisely what he does at that particular moment. Consequently the entire empirical course of a man's life is, in great things and in small, as necessarily predetermined as clockwork. The fundamental reason this is so is that the mode in which the metaphysical free act referred to enters the knowing consciousness is that of perception, the form of which is space and time; through the agency of space and time the unity and indivisibility of this act from then on appears drawn out into a series of states and occurrences which take place in accordance with the principle of sufficient reason in its four forms, this being precisely what is meant by *necessity*. The outcome however is a moral one, namely this, that by what we do we know what we are, just as by what we suffer we know what we deserve.

8

The question has been raised what two men who have grown up entirely alone in the desert would do when they met one another for the first time. Hobbes, Pufendorf and Rousseau have given quite different answers to this question. Pufendorf believed they would approach one another affectionately; Hobbes, that they would be hostile; Rousseau, that they would pass one another by in silence. All three are both right and wrong: the *immeasurable difference between the inborn moral disposition of one individual and another* would in precisely this situation reveal itself in so clear a light that such a meeting would be, as it were, a standard of measurement of this disposition. In some men the sight of other men at once arouses a hostile feeling, in that their inmost being declares: 'Not me!' There are others in whom it at once arouses a friendly interest: their inmost being says: 'Me once more!' Countless gradations lie between these two extremes. – But that we differ so fundamentally on this cardinal point is a great problem, indeed a mystery.

9

It is a wonderful thing how the *individuality* of *every* man (i.e. a certain particular character with a certain particular intellect) minutely determines his every thought and action and like a penetrative dye permeates even the most insignificant part of them, so that the entire life-course, i.e. the inner and outer history, of each one differs fundamentally from that of all the others. As a botanist can recognize the whole plant from one leaf, as Cuvier can construct the whole animal from one bone, so an accurate knowledge of a man's character can be arrived at from a single characteristic action; and that is true even when this action involves some trifle – indeed this is often better for the purpose, for with important things people are on their guard, while with trifles they follow their own nature without much reflection.

The true basis and propaedeutic for all knowledge of human nature is the persuasion that a man's actions are, essentially and as a whole, not directed by his reason and its designs; so that no one becomes this or that because he wants to, though he want to never so much, but that his conduct proceeds from his inborn and inalterable character, is more narrowly and in particulars determined by motivation, and is thus necessarily the product of these two factors.

If you grasp this you will also see that we can really never make more than a supposition about what we will do in any future situation, although we often think we have made a decision about it. If, e.g., a man undertakes to do this or that should certain circumstances arise in the future, and gives this undertaking with the firmest intention of carrying it out, even with the liveliest desire to carry it out, this does not by any means ensure that he *will* carry it out, unless he is so constituted that his given promise itself and as such becomes a constantly sufficient motivation, so that with regard to his honour it operates on him like an external compulsion. What he will actually do when these circumstances arise can, moreover, be predicted only from a true and perfect knowledge of his character and of the external circumstances under whose influence he has then come; although if these conditions were met, it could be predicted with absolute certainty. The unalterability of our character and the necessary nature of our actions will be brought home with uncommon force to anyone who has on any occasion behaved as he ought not to have behaved, who has been lacking in resolution or constancy or courage or some other quality demanded by the circumstances of the moment. Afterwards he honestly recognizes and regrets his failing, and no doubt thinks: 'I'll do better another time.' Another time comes, the circumstances are repeated, and he does as he did before – to his great astonishment.

The best illustration of the truth here under discussion is provided in general by the plays of Shakespeare. For he was thoroughly convinced of it and his intuitive wisdom expresses itself *in concreto* on all sides. I would like to exemplify it, however, with a case in which he emphasizes it with particular clarity: I mean the character of the Earl of Northumberland, whom we see traverse three tragedies without ever really taking a major role in the drama but, on the contrary, appearing in only a few scenes spread over fifteen acts; so that unless you give it all your attention you can easily lose sight of the moral consistency of his character, though the poet never lost sight of it. Whenever Northumberland appears Shakespeare allows him a noble, knightly demeanour and gives him language appropriate to it – indeed, he sometimes has very beautiful and even sublime passages to speak, since Shakespeare's practice is very far removed from that of Schiller, who likes to paint the Devil black and whose moral approval or disapproval of the characters he is drawing is audible in the words they themselves speak. In the case of Shakespeare, as also in that of Goethe, every character is, while he stands and speaks, entirely in the right, though he be the Devil himself. Compare in this respect Goethe's Duke of Alba with Schiller's. We first make the acquaintance of the Earl of Northumberland in *Richard II*, where he is the first to plot against the king in favour of Bolingbroke, later Henry IV, whom he has earlier (Act III, scene 3) personally flattered. In the following act he is reproved for referring to the king simply as Richard, which however he asserts he did merely for the sake of brevity. Soon afterwards it is his insidious speech which persuades the king to capitulate. In the following act, in the scene in which he abdicates, Northumberland treats him with such disdain and harshness that the unhappy broken monarch for once loses his patience and cries: 'Fiend, thou torment'st me ere I come to hell!' At the end of the play he informs the new king that he has sent the severed heads of his predecessor's followers to London. – In the following tragedy, *Henry IV*, he plots against the new king in the same way as he did against the old. In the fourth act we see the rebels joined together preparing for the following day's decisive battle and impatiently awaiting the arrival only of him and his forces. At length a letter arrives from him: he himself is sick but he cannot entrust his forces to another; nonetheless, they should courageously proceed with the business and go bravely to battle. This they do: but, decidedly weakened by his absence, they are totally defeated, most of their leaders are captured, and Northumberland's own son, the valiant Hotspur, falls at the hands of the Crown Prince. – We see him again in the following play, the second part of *Henry IV*, where he is wild with rage at the death of his son and breathing the most fearful vengeance, in pursuit of which he incites renewed rebellion. Its leaders again assemble; as they are preparing, in the fourth act, to give the decisive battle and are waiting only for him to join them, a letter arrives: he has been unable to collect together a sufficient force, so he intends for the present to seek safety in Scotland; nonetheless, he sincerely wishes them every success in their valiant undertaking. Whereupon they surrender to the king under a pact which the king fails to honour, and thus perish.

The Fate of the ancients is nothing other than the conscious certainty that all events are bound firmly together by the chain of causality and thus occur with strict necessity, so that the future is already totally fixed and precisely determined, and can no more be altered than the past can.

On Psychology

1

The *will* to live, which constitutes the inmost kernel of every living thing, appears most unconcealedly in the higher, that is to say cleverest animals, and its nature may in them consequently be observed most plainly. *Beneath* this stage it does not appear so clearly, has a lower degree of objectivization; *above* it, however – that is to say, in man – the presence of reason means the existence of circumspection, and with it the capacity for dissimulation, which straightway throws a veil over the will. Here the will therefore steps out unconcealed only in outbursts of emotion and passion: and this is why when passion speaks it always, and rightly, inspires belief, no matter what passion it may be. It is for the same reason that the passions are the principal theme of the poets and the actors' showpiece. – It is on the previously mentioned fact, however, that our pleasure in dogs, monkeys, cats, etc., depends: it is the perfect *naïveté* of all their actions which so delights us.

2

Many things attributed to *force of habit* depend rather on the constancy and unalterability of our primary and inborn character, in consequence of which under similar circumstances we always do the *same* thing, with the same necessity the hundredth time as the first time. – Genuine *force of habit*, on the other hand, really derives from the *inertia* which wants to spare the intellect and the will the labour, difficulty and sometimes the danger involved in making a fresh choice, and which therefore lets us do today what we did yesterday and a hundred times before that, and what we know will meet the case.

The truth of the matter, however, lies deeper: for it is to be understood in a more particular sense than seems to be the case at first sight. That which is to the body in so far as it is activated by purely mechanical causes the *force of inertia*, is to the body which is moved by motivations the *force of habit*. The actions we perform out of pure habit really occur without any individual, special motivation, which is why we do not really think about them while we are performing them. Only the first instance of any action which has become a habit was motivated: the secondary after-effect of this motivation constitutes the present habit, which suffices to perpetuate the action in the same way as a body which has been set in motion by a thrust needs no further thrust to keep it in motion but will go on for all eternity provided it encounters no obstruction. The same applies to animals, in that their training is an enforced habit. The horse passively pulls its cart on and on without being driven: this motion is still the effect of the blow of the whip which first sent it off, perpetuated as habit according to the law of inertia. – All this is really more than a mere metaphor: the things are identical – they are the will at very different stages of its objectivization, which just because it conforms with the same law of motion assumes such differing shapes.

3

Viva muchos años! is a common greeting in Spanish, and the wish for long life is very customary all over the world. This is no doubt to be explained, not by a knowledge of what life is like, but of what man is like in his intrinsic nature – namely the will to live.

4

Every parting is a foretaste of death, and every reunion a foretaste of resurrection. That is why even people who were indifferent to one another rejoice so much when they meet again after twenty or thirty years.

5

The reason the sudden announcement of a great piece of good fortune can easily prove fatal is that happiness and unhappiness is no more than the ratio between what we demand and what we receive, so that we are not sensible of the goods we possess or are quite certain of possessing as such; because all enjoyment is really only *negative*, only has the effect of removing a pain, while pain or evil, on the other hand, is the actual positive element and is felt directly. With possession, or the certain prospect of it, our demands straightway increase and this increases our capacity for further possessions and wider prospects. If, on the contrary, constant misfortune has contracted our spirit and reduced our demands to a minimum, we lack the capacity to receive a sudden piece of good fortune; for since it meets with no existing demands which neutralize it, it produces an apparently positive effect and thus acts with its full force: so that it can burst the spirit asunder, i.e. prove fatal.

6

Hope is the confusion of the desire for a thing with its probability.

He who is without hope is also without fear: this is the meaning of the expression 'desperate'. For it is natural to man to believe true what he desires to be true, and to believe it because he desires it; if this salutary and soothing quality in his nature is obliterated by repeated ill-fortune, and he is even brought to the point of believing that what he does not desire to happen must happen and what he desires to happen can never happen simply because he desires it, then this is the condition called despair.

7

There is an unconscious appositeness in the use of the word *person* to designate the human individual, as is done in all European languages: for *persona* really means an actor's mask, and it is true that no one reveals himself as he is; we all wear a mask and play a role.

8

When he suffers an injustice the natural man burns with a thirst for *revenge*, and it has often been said that revenge is sweet. This fact is confirmed by the many sacrifices that have been made simply for the sake of revenge and without any idea of gaining recompense. I should like to attempt a psychological explanation of this.

No suffering laid upon us by nature or chance or fate is so painful as that inflicted by the will of another. This is so because we recognize nature and chance as the primal masters of the world and we can see that what nature and chance do to us they would have done to anyone else, so that when our sufferings originate from this source what we bewail is rather the common lot of man than our own individual lot. Suffering caused by the will of another, on the other hand, includes a quite peculiar and bitter addition to the pain or injury itself, namely the consciousness of someone else's superiority, whether in point of strength or of cunning, together with that of one's own impotence. Recompense, if recompense is possible, can cure the injury done: but that bitter addition, the feeling 'and that is what I have to put up with from you' which often hurts more than the injury itself, can be neutralized only by revenge. By returning the injury, either by force or by cunning, we demonstrate our superiority over him who has injured us and thereby annul the proof he gave of his superiority over us. Thus the heart acquires the satisfaction it thirsted for. Where, consequently, there is much pride or much vanity there will also be much revengefulness. But, as every fulfilled desire reveals itself more or less as a delusion, so does that for revenge. Usually the pleasure we hoped for from it is made bitter by the pity we afterwards feel; indeed, an exacted revenge will often subsequently break the heart and torment the conscience: we no longer feel the motivation which drove us to it, but the proof of our wickedness remains visibly before us.

9

Money is human happiness *in abstracto*; consequently he who is no longer capable of happiness *in concreto* sets his whole heart on money.

10

When will crowds out knowledge we call the result *obstinacy*.

11

Hatred is a thing of the heart, *contempt* a thing of the head.

Hatred and contempt are decidedly antagonistic towards one another and mutually exclusive. A great deal of hatred, indeed, has no other source than a compelled respect for the superior qualities of some other person; conversely, if you were to consider hating every miserable wretch you met you would have your work cut out: it is much easier to despise them one and all. True, genuine contempt, which is the obverse of true, genuine pride, stays hidden away in secret and lets no one suspect its existence: for if you let a person you despise notice the fact, you thereby reveal a certain respect for him, inasmuch as you want him to know how low you rate him – which betrays not contempt but hatred, which excludes contempt and only affects it. Genuine contempt, on the other hand, is the unsullied conviction of the worthlessness of another; it permits of indulgence and forbearance, in that for the sake of one's own peace and security one refrains from provoking the person despised, since everyone is capable of causing injury. If, however, this pure, cold and sincere contempt does ever reveal itself, it is requited with the most sanguinary hatred, because it is not within the power of the person despised to requite it with contempt.

12

What makes men *hard-hearted* is that everyone has sufficient troubles of his own to bear, or thinks he has. What, on the other hand, makes them so *inquisitive* is the polar opposite of suffering – boredom.

13

If you want to know how you really feel about someone take note of the impression an unexpected letter from him makes on you when you first see it on the doormat.

14

Reason deserves also to be called a *prophet*, for it holds the future up to us (namely as the coming consequence and effect of what we are now doing). This is precisely why it is calculated to keep us in check when lustful desires or outbursts of rage or avariciousness threaten to mislead us into courses which we would later be bound to regret.

15

States of human happiness and good fortune can as a rule be compared with certain groups of trees: seen from a distance they look beautiful, but if you go up to and into them their beauty disappears and you can no longer discover it. That is why we so often feel envy for other people.

16

Why, despite all our mirrors, do we never really know what we look like, and consequently cannot picture ourselves in imagination, as we can everyone else we know?

The reason is undoubtedly in part the fact that when we look at ourselves in a mirror we always do so with a direct and unmoving gaze, whereby the play of the eyes, which is so meaningful and in fact the actual characteristic of our gaze, is in great part lost. With this physical impossibility, however, there seems to go an analogous ethical impossibility. The condition under which *objective* comprehension of something perceived is possible is *alienation* from that which is perceived; but when we see our own reflection in a mirror we are unable to take an alienated view of it, because this view depends ultimately on moral egoism, with its profound feeling of *not me*: so that when we see our own reflection our egoism whispers to us a precautionary 'This is not not-me, but me', which has the effect of a *noli me tangere* and prevents any purely objective comprehension.

17

Unconscious existence possesses reality only for other beings in whose consciousness it appears: *immediate* reality is conditional upon individual consciousness. Thus the individual real existence of man also lies first and foremost in his *consciousness*. But this is as such necessarily ideational, and thus conditioned by the intellect and by the sphere and substance of the intellect's activity. The degree of clarity of consciousness, and consequently of thought, can therefore be regarded as the degree of *reality of existence*. But this degree of thought, or of clear consciousness of one's own existence and of that of others, varies very greatly within the human race itself according to the measure of natural intellectual power, the extent to which this has been developed, and the amount of leisure available for reflection.

So far as intrinsic and inborn differences in intellectual power are concerned, these cannot very well be compared without considering each individual case, because such differences are not visible from a distance and not so easily discernible as distinctions in respect of culture, leisure and employment. But even going by these alone, it has to be admitted that many a man possesses at least a tenfold greater *degree of existence* than another – *exists* ten times as much.

There is no need to speak of savages whose life is often no more than one stage above that of the apes in the trees: consider for instance a porter in Naples or

Venice (in the north the need to guard against the winter already makes men more thoughtful), and regard the course of his life from its beginning to its end. Driven by want, sustained by his own strength, supplying the needs of the day, indeed of the hour, through his own labour; a great deal of exertion, constant turmoil, a great deal of hardship; no care for the morrow, refreshing rest after exhaustion, much wrangling and brawling, not a moment to spare for reflection, sensual ease in a mild climate and with tolerable food; finally, as the metaphysical element, some crass superstition provided by the Church. This restless, confused dream constitutes the life of millions of men. They *know* only for the purposes of their present *wants*: they give no thought to the coherence of their existence, not to speak of that of existence itself: to a certain extent they exist without really being aware of it.

Now consider the prudent, sensible merchant, who passes his life in speculations, cautiously carries out well-considered plans, establishes his house, makes provision for wife, child and heirs and also takes an active part in public affairs. This man obviously exists with very much more consciousness than the former: i.e. his existence possesses a higher degree of reality.

Next, observe the scholar, one for instance who explores the history of the past. This man will be conscious of the existence of the whole, beyond the era of his own existence, beyond his own person: he ponders the course of the world.

And finally the poet, and even more the philosopher, in whom thought has attained such a degree that, neglecting individual phenomena *in* existence, he stands in wonder before *existence itself*, before this mighty sphinx, and makes of it his problem. Consciousness has in him risen to such a degree of clarity that it has become universal consciousness, through which in him idea has stepped beyond all relation to the service of his will and now holds up to him a world which challenges him rather to investigation and contemplation than to involvement in its activities. – If, now, degrees of consciousness are degrees of reality – then when we call such a man the 'most real being' the phrase will have sense and meaning.

18

Why is 'common' an expression of contempt? 'uncommon, exceptional' one of approval? Why is everything common contemptible?

The original meaning of *common* is that which pertains to all, i.e. to the entire species. Consequently, he who possesses no further qualities than those pertaining to the human species in general is a *common man*.

For what value can be possessed by a being which is no different from millions of his kind? Millions? an infinity rather, an endless number of beings ceaselessly spurted forth by nature out of its inexhaustible well *in saecula saeculorum* [to all eternity], as generous with them as the blacksmith is with sparks.

I have often argued that, while animals possess only a species character, man alone receives an actual individual character. Yet in most people there is only very little that is truly individual: they can be almost entirely divided into classes. Their desires and thoughts, like their faces, are those of the whole species, or at any rate of the class of man to which they belong, and are for that very reason trivial, everyday, common, thousandfold repeated. What they say and do can likewise usually be predicted in advance with a fair degree of accuracy. They have no individual quality: they are factory-made.

As their being is comprised in that of the species, should their existence not be so too? What goes without saying, however, is that every lofty, great, noble being will in consequence of his nature stand isolated in a world in which, to designate what is low and objectionable, no better expression could be found than that which means of ordinary occurrence: 'common'.

19

The will, as the thing in itself, is the common stuff of all beings, the universal element of things: consequently we possess it in common with each and every man, indeed with the animals, and even further on down. In the will as such we are consequently all similar, in so far as everything and everyone is filled and distended with will. On the other hand, that which exalts being above being, man above man, is knowledge. For that reason what we say should as far as possible be limited to expressions of knowledge. For the *will*, as that which is *common* to all, is for that reason also *common*: consequently, every vehement emergence of will is *common*, i.e. it demeans us to a mere exemplar of the species, for we then exhibit only the character of the species. What is common therefore is all anger, unbounded joy, all hatred, all fear, in short every emotion, i.e. every agitation of the will, if it becomes so strong as decisively to preponderate over knowledge in the consciousness and to allow a man to appear more as a willing than a knowing being. If he surrenders to such an emotion the greatest genius becomes equal to the commonest son of earth. He, on the other hand, who wants to be altogether uncommon, that is to say great, must never let a preponderant agitation of will take his consciousness over altogether, however much he is urged to do so. He must, e.g., be able to take note of the odious opinion of another without feeling his own aroused by it: indeed, there is no surer sign of greatness than ignoring hurtful or insulting expressions by attributing them without further ado, like countless other errors, to the speaker's lack of knowledge and thus merely taking note of them without feeling them.

20

Everything primary, and consequently everything genuine, in man works as the forces of nature do, *unconsciously*. What has passed through the consciousness thereby becomes an idea: consequently the expression of it is to a certain extent the communication of an idea. It follows that all the genuine and proved qualities of the character and the mind are primarily unconscious and only as such do they make a deep impression. What man performs unconsciously costs him no effort, and no effort can provide a substitute for it: it is in this fashion that all original conceptions such as lie at the bottom of every genuine achievement and constitute its kernel come into being. Thus only what is inborn is genuine and sound: if you want to achieve something in business, in writing, in painting, in anything, you must *follow the rules without knowing them.*

21

Many undoubtedly owe their good fortune to the circumstance that they possess a pleasing smile with which they win hearts. Yet these hearts would do better to beware and to learn from Hamlet's tables that one may smile, and smile, and be a villain.

22

People with great and splendid qualities make very little ado about admitting their faults and weaknesses. They regard them as something they have paid for, or they even go so far as to think that, far from being shamed by such weaknesses, they are doing these weaknesses honour by possessing them. This will especially be the case when these faults are those which go with their great qualities, as *conditiones sine quibus non.* As George Sand says: *chacun a les défauts de ses vertus.*

On the other hand, there are people of good character and irreproachable intelligence who never admit their few minor weaknesses, but carefully conceal them rather and are very sensitive to any allusion to them: the reason is that their whole merit lies in the absence of faults and defects, so that every fault that comes to light directly diminishes it.

23

If your abilities are only mediocre, *modesty* is mere honesty; but if you possess great talents, it is hypocrisy.

24

Man excels all the animals even in his *ability to be trained*. Moslems are trained to turn their faces towards Mecca five times a day and pray: they do so steadfastly. Christians are trained to cross themselves on certain occasions, to genuflect, etc.; while religion in general constitutes the real masterpiece in the art of training, namely the training of the mental capacities – which, as is well known, cannot be started too early. There is no absurdity so palpable that one could not fix it firmly in the head of every man on earth provided one began to imprint it before his sixth year by ceaselessly rehearsing it before him with solemn earnestness. For the training of men, as of animals, can be completely successful only in early youth.

25

To possess a great deal of *imagination* means that the *perceiving function of the brain* is sufficiently strong not invariably to require stimulation by the senses in order to become active.

The imagination is, consequently, the more active the fewer perceptions from without are transmitted to us by the senses. Protracted solitude, in prison or in a sick-bed, silence, twilight, darkness are conducive to it: under their influence it comes into play without being summoned. On the other hand, when a great deal of real material is provided from without for us to perceive, as on journeys, in the bustle of life, at high noon, then the imagination takes a holiday and refuses to become active even when summoned: it sees that this is not its season.

Nonetheless, if the imagination is to be fruitful it must have received a great deal of material from the outer world, for this alone can fill its store-room. But the nourishing of the fantasy is like the nourishing of the body: it is precisely at the time it is being given a great deal of nourishment which it has to digest that the body is at its least efficient and most likes to take a holiday – yet it is to this nourishment that it owes all the strength which later, in the right season, it manifests.

26

The *memory* may well become confused by what is put into it, but it cannot really become surfeited. Its capacity is not reduced by receiving, any more than arranging sand into different shapes reduces its capacity to receive other shapes. In this sense the memory is bottomless. Yet the more knowledge you possess, and the more multifarious it is, the more time you will require to find in your memory precisely what it is you want, because you will then be like a storekeeper who is trying to find one particular article in a large, variously stocked store; or, to speak correctly, because out of the very large number of trains of thought possible to you, you have to call up precisely *that* train which by virtue of previous exercise leads to the desired memory. For the memory is not a store-room for preserving things, it is only the capacity for exercising the mental powers: the head possesses knowledge only *potentia*, not *actu*.

27

People of very great ability will as a rule get on better with people of very limited ability than they will with people of ordinary ability, for the same reason as the despot and the plebeian, the grandparents and the grand-children are natural allies.

People need external activity because they have no internal activity. Where, on the contrary, the latter does exist, the former is likely to be a very troublesome, indeed execrable annoyance and impediment. – The former fact also explains the restlessness of those who have nothing to do, and their aimless travelling. What drives them from country to country is the same boredom which at home drives them together into such crowds and heaps it is funny to see. I once received a choice confirmation of this truth from a gentleman of 50 with whom I was not acquainted, who told me about a two-year pleasure trip he had taken to distant lands and strange parts of the earth. When I remarked that he must have endured many difficulties, hardships and dangers, he replied very naïvely, without hesitation or preamble but as if merely enunciating the conclusion of a syllogism: 'I wasn't bored for an instant.'

On Religion

1

Faith and Knowledge. Philosophy, as a science, has nothing whatever to do with what should or may be *believed*, it has to do only with what can be *known*. If this should turn out to be something quite other than what one is supposed to believe that is no disadvantage even for the belief, since it is the nature of belief to teach what cannot be known. If it could be known, belief would be ludicrous and useless: it would be, for instance, as if one should propound a theory to be held by faith in the field of mathematics.

It can, on the other hand, be objected that faith can teach more, much more, than philosophy; yet it can teach nothing which could be combined with the conclusion of philosophy, because knowledge is of a harder stuff than faith, so that when they collide the latter is shattered.

In any event, faith and knowledge are totally different things which for their mutual benefit have to be kept strictly separate, so that each goes its own way without paying the slightest attention to the other.

2

Revelation. The ephemeral generations of man are born and pass away in quick succession; individual men, burdened with fear, want and sorrow, dance into the arms of death. As they do so they never weary of asking what it is that ails them and what the whole tragi-comedy is supposed to mean. They call on Heaven for an answer, but Heaven stays silent. Instead of a voice from Heaven there come along priests with revelations.

But he is still in his childhood who can think that superhuman beings have ever given our race information about the aim of its existence or that of the world. There are no other revelations than the thoughts of the wise, even if these – subject to error, as are all things human – are often clothed in strange allegories and myths and are then called religions. To this extent, therefore, it is all one whether you live and die trusting in your own thoughts or in those of others, for you are never trusting in anything but human thoughts and human opinion. Yet as a rule men have a weakness for putting their trust in those who pretend to supernatural sources of knowledge rather than in their own heads; but if you bear in mind the enormous intellectual inequality between man and man, then the thoughts of one may very well count with another as a revelation.

The fundamental, secret and primal piece of astuteness of all priests, everywhere and at all times, whether Brahmin or Mohammedan or Buddhist or Christian, is as follows. They have recognized and grasped the enormous strength and the ineradicability of the metaphysical need of man: they then pretend to possess the means of satisfying it, in that the solution to the great enigma has, by extraordinary channels, been directly communicated to them. Once they have persuaded men of the truth of this, they can lead and dominate them to their heart's content. The more prudent rulers enter into an alliance with them: the others are themselves ruled by them. If, however, as the rarest of all exceptions, a philosopher comes to the throne, the whole comedy is disrupted in the most unseemly fashion.

3

On Christianity. To arrive at a just judgement of Christianity one must consider what preceded it and what it supplanted. First and foremost Graeco-Roman paganism: considered as popular metaphysics a very trivial affair, without any real, distinct dogmas, without any categorical ethic, indeed without any real moral tendency, and without sacred scriptures: so that it hardly deserves to be called a religion at all – it is rather a play of fantasy, a production cobbled together by poets out of popular legends, and for the most part an obvious personification of natural forces. It is hard to imagine that grown men ever took this childish religion seriously: yet there are many passages in ancient writers which suggest that they did, notably the first book of Valerius Maximus but even a good many passages in Herodotus. In later times and with the advance of philosophy such serious credence vanished, which made it possible for Christianity to supplant this state religion in spite of its external supports. – The second thing Christianity had to supplant was Judaism, whose rude dogma was sublimated and tacitly allegorized in the Christian. Christianity is in general definitely of an allegorical nature: for what in profane matters is called allegory is in religions called mystery. It has to be conceded that Christianity is much superior to both these earlier religions not only as regards *morality*, in which it alone (so far as the Occident is concerned) teaches *caritas*, reconciliation, love of one's enemy, resignation and denial of one's own will, but even as regards *dogma*: it is best, however, to communicate this to the great masses, who are incapable of grasping truth directly, in the form of a beautiful allegory, which completely suffices them as a guide to practical living and as an anchor of consolation and hope. But a small addition of absurdity is a necessary ingredient in such an allegory: it serves to indicate its allegorical nature. If you take Christian dogma *sensu proprio*, then Voltaire is right. Taken allegorically, on the other hand, it is a sacred myth, a vehicle for bringing to the people truths which would otherwise be altogether inaccessible to them. Even the Church's assertion that reason is totally incompetent and blind with respect to the dogmas of religion and must be repudiated means at bottom that these dogmas are of an allegorical nature and therefore not to be judged by the standards which reason, which takes everything *sensu proprio*, can alone apply. The absurdities of dogma are precisely the mark and sign of the allegorical and mythical, even though in the present case they

arise from the need to link together two such heterogeneous doctrines as those of the Old and the New
Testaments. This great allegory first came about gradually through the interpretation of external and chance
circumstances under the silent influence of a deep-lying
truth not clearly present in the consciousness, until it
was finally completed by Augustine, who penetrated
most deeply into its meaning and was then able to
comprehend it as a systematic whole and to supply what
was lacking in it. Thus the complete and perfect Christian
doctrine is that of Augustine, as also affirmed by Luther,
and not, as present-day Protestants who, taking 'revelation' *sensu proprio* confine it to *one* individual, think,
primitive Christianity – (just as it is not the seed but the
fruit which is edible). – Yet the weak point of all religions
remains that they can never dare to confess to being
allegorical, so that they have to present their doctrines
in all seriousness as true *sensu proprio*; which, because of
the absurdities essential to allegory, leads to perpetual
deception and a great disadvantage for religion. What is
even worse, indeed, is that in time it comes to light that
they are *not* true *sensu proprio*, and then they perish. To
this extent it would be better to admit their allegorical
nature straightway: only the difficulty here is to make
the people understand that a thing can be true and not
true at the same time. But since we find that all religions
are constituted to a greater or less degree in this way,
we have to recognize that the absurd is to a certain
extent appropriate to the human race, indeed an element
of its life, and that deception is indispensable to it – a fact
which is confirmed in other directions.

Evidence for and an example of the above-mentioned origin of absurdities in the union of the Old Testament and the New is provided by, among other things, the Christian doctrine of predestination and grace perfected by Luther's guiding star, Augustine: according to this doctrine one man has the advantage over another of being the object of divine grace, which amounts to coming into the world possessed of a ready-made privilege, and one in respect of the most important matter of all. The offensiveness and absurdity of this doctrine originates, however, entirely in the presupposition, derived from the Old Testament, that man is the work of an external will, which called him up out of nothing. But considering that genuine moral superiority actually is inborn, the matter appears in a quite different and more rational light under the Brahmanic and Buddhist presupposition of metempsychosis, according to which whatever advantages a man may be born with he has brought with him from another world and an earlier life, so that they are not a gift of grace but the fruit of his own deeds performed in that other world. – To this dogma of Augustine there is, however, joined this worse one, that out of the mass of mankind, who are corrupt and thus doomed to everlasting damnation, a very small number are, as a consequence of predestination and election by grace, acquitted and will consequently be saved, while deserved destruction and the eternal torments of Hell will be visited on the rest. Taken *sensu proprio* the dogma here becomes revolting, for not only does it punish the faults, or even the mere lack of faith, of a life often hardly more than twenty years long with torments which have no end, it also adds that this almost universal damnation is actually the effect of original sin, and thus the necessary consequence of man's first Fall. But this must have been foreseen by at any rate him who firstly failed to make men better than they are and then set a trap for them into which he must have known they would fall, since everything was his work and nothing was hidden from him. According to this dogma, then, he called into existence out of nothing a weak and sin-prone race in order to hand it over to endless torment. There is finally the further fact that the God who pre-scribes forbearance and forgiveness of every sin, even to the point of loving one's enemy, fails to practise it himself, but does rather the opposite: since a punishment which is introduced at the end of things, when all is over and done with for ever, can be intended neither to improve nor deter; it is nothing but revenge. Thus regarded, it seems that the entire race is in fact definitely intended and expressly created for eternal torment and damnation – all, that is, apart from those few exceptions which are rescued from this fate by divine grace, although one knows not why. These aside, it appears as if the dear Lord created the world for the benefit of the Devil – in which event he would have done far better not to have created it at all. – This is what happens to dogmas when you take them *sensu proprio*: understood *sensu allegorico*, on the other hand, all this is susceptible of a more satisfactory interpretation. What is absurd, indeed revolting, in this doctrine is however, as has already been said, first and foremost merely a conse-quence of Judaic theism, with its creation from nothing and that which goes with it, the really paradoxical and scandalous denial of the natural doctrine of metempsychosis, a doctrine which is to a certain extent self-evident and which has therefore been in all ages accepted by virtually the entire human race with the exception of the Jews. It was precisely to obviate the colossal disadvantage arising from this rejection of metempsychosis and to moderate the revolting nature of the dogma that in the sixth century Pope Gregory I very wisely developed the doctrine of Purgatory (which is, in its essentials, to be found as early as Origen) and formally incorporated it into the teaching of the Church; whereby a kind of substitute for metempsychosis was introduced into Christianity, inasmuch as both constitute a process of purification. It was with the same objective in view that the doctrine of the restoration of all things was instituted, according to which even the sinners are one and all restituted *in integrum* in the last act of the universal comedy. Only the Protestants, with their obstinate Bible religion, have refused to let themselves be deprived of everlasting punishment in Hell. Much good may it do 'em – one might say maliciously: the consolation is, however, that they do not really believe in it; for the moment they are leaving that subject alone, thinking in their hearts: Oh, it won't be as bad as all that.

The Augustinian conception of the enormous number of the sinners and the very small number of those who deserve eternal bliss, which is in itself a correct conception, is also to be discovered in Brahmanism and Buddhism, where, however, the doctrine of metempsychosis robs it of its repellent character. It is true that in the former final redemption and in the latter Nirvana is also granted to very few, but these do not come into the world specially chosen and privileged, their deserts are those they have acquired in a previous life and which they continue to maintain in the present one. The rest, however, are not cast into the everlasting pit of Hell, they are transported to the kind of world which is in keeping with their deeds. If, consequently, you should ask the propounders of these religions where and what all those who have not attained to redemption are, they would reply: 'Look around you: here is where they are, this is what they are: this is their arena, this is Sansara, i.e. the world of desire, of birth, of pain, of age, of sickness and of death.' – On the other hand, if this Augustinian dogma of the tiny number of the elect and the great number of the eternally damned is understood merely *sensu allegorico* and interpreted in the sense of our own philosophy, then it agrees with the fact that only very few achieve denial of the will and thereby redemption from this world (as in Buddhism only very few achieve Nirvana). What, on the other hand, this dogma hypostatizes as eternal damnation is nothing other than this world of ours: *this* is what devolves upon all the rest. It is a sufficiently evil place: it is Purgatory, it is Hell, and devils are not lacking in it. Only consider what men sometimes inflict upon men, with what ingenious torments one will slowly torture another to death, and ask yourself whether devils could do more. And sojourn in this place is likewise eternal for all those who obdurately persist in affirming the will to live.

But in truth, if one from Asia should ask me what Europe is, I would have to reply: it is the continent utterly possessed by the unheard-of and incredible delusion that the birth of man is his absolute beginning and that he is created out of nothing.

Fundamentally, and both their mythologies apart, Buddha's *Sansara* and *Nirvana* are identical with Augustine's two *civitates* into which the world is divided, the *civitas terrena* and *coelestis* [The city of this world and the city of God].

The *Devil* is in Christianity a very necessary personage, as counterweight to the all-goodness, omniscience and omnipotence of God: it is impossible to see where the predominating, incalculable and boundless evil of the world is supposed to come from if the Devil is not there to assume responsibility for it. Since the Rationalists have abolished him, the disadvantage to the other side accruing from his absence has grown greater and greater and more and more evident: which could have been foreseen and was foreseen by the orthodox. For you cannot remove one pillar from a building without endangering the rest. – This also confirms what has been established elsewhere, that Jehovah is a transformation of Ormuzd and Satan of Ahriman, who is inseparable from him: Ormuzd himself, however, is a transformation of Indra.

Christianity possesses the peculiar disadvantage that, unlike the other religions, it is not a pure *doctrine*, but essentially and above all a *history*, a succession of events, a complex of facts and the actions and sufferings of individuals, and it is this history which constitutes the dogma belief in which redeems.

Another fundamental error of Christianity is that it has in an unnatural fashion sundered mankind from the *animal world* to which it essentially belongs and now considers mankind alone as of any account, regarding the animals as no more than *things*. This error is a consequence of creation out of nothing, after which the Creator, in the first and second chapters of Genesis, takes all the animals just as if they were things, and without so much as the recommendation to kind treatment which even a dog-seller usually adds when he parts with his dogs, hands them over to man for man to *rule*, that is to do with them what he likes; subsequently, in the second chapter, the Creator goes on to appoint him the first professor of zoology by commissioning him to give the animals the names they shall thenceforth bear, which is once more only a symbol of their total dependence on him, i.e. their total lack of rights.

It can truly be said: Men are the devils of the earth, and the animals are the tormented souls. This is the consequence of that installation scene in the Garden of Eden. For the mob can be controlled only by force or by religion, and here Christianity leaves us shamefully in the lurch. I heard from a reliable source that a Protestant pastor, requested by an animal protection society to preach a sermon against cruelty to animals, replied that with the best will in the world he was unable to do so, because he could find no support in his religion. The man was honest, and he was right.

When I was studying at Göttingen, Blumenbach spoke to us very seriously about the horrors of vivisection and told us what a cruel and terrible thing it was; wherefore it should be resorted to only very seldom and for very important experiments which would bring immediate benefit, and even then it must be carried out as publicly as possible so that the cruel sacrifice on the altar of science should be of the maximum possible usefulness. Nowadays, on the contrary, every little medicine-man thinks he has the right to torment animals in the cruellest fashion in his torture chamber so as to decide problems whose answers have for long stood written in books into which he is too lazy and ignorant to stick his nose. – Special mention should be made of an abomination committed by Baron Ernst von Bibra at Nürnberg and, with incomprehensible *naïveté, tanquam re bene gesta* [As if the thing were done well], narrated by him to the public in his *Vergleichende Untersuchungen über das Gehirn des Menschen und der Wirbelthiere*: he deliberately let two rabbits *starve to death!* – in order to undertake the totally idle and useless experiment of seeing whether starvation produces a proportional change in the chemical composition of the brain! For the ends of science – *n'est-ce pas?* Have these gentlemen of the scalpel and crucible no notion at all then that they are first and foremost men, and chemists only secondly? How can you sleep soundly knowing you have harmless animals under lock and key in order to starve them slowly to death? Don't you wake up screaming in the night?

It is obviously high time that the Jewish conception of nature, at any rate in regard to animals, should come to an end in Europe, and that *the eternal being which, as it lives in us, also lives in every animal* should be recognized as such, and as such treated with care and consideration. One must be blind, deaf and dumb, or completely chloroformed by the *foetor judaicus*, not to see that the animal is in essence absolutely the same thing that we are, and that the difference lies merely in the accident, the intellect, and not in the substance, which is the will.

The greatest benefit conferred by the railways is that they spare millions of draught-horses their miserable existence.

4

On Theism. Just as polytheism is the personification of individual departments and forces of nature, so monotheism is the personification of the whole of nature at one blow.

But when I try to imagine myself standing before an individual being and saying to him: 'My creator! Once I was nothing: but you have brought me forth, so that now I am something, and what that something is is myself' – and then adding: 'Thank you for this favour' – and even concluding with: 'If I have been good for nothing, that is *my* fault' – then I must confess that, as a consequence of my philosophical and Indian studies, my head has become incapable of sustaining such a thought. And this thought is moreover a counterpart of that which Kant presents us in the *Critique of Pure Reason* (in the section on the impossibility of a cosmological proof): 'One cannot resist the thought, although neither can one endure it, that a being which we imagine as the highest of all possible beings says as it were to himself: I am from eternity to eternity, there is nothing beside me except what exists purely through my will: *but whence am I then?*'

It is all one whether you make an idol of wood, stone, metal, or put it together out of abstract concepts: as soon as you have before you a personal being to whom you sacrifice, on whom you call, whom you thank, it is *idolatry*. It also makes little difference at bottom whether you sacrifice your sheep or your inclinations. Every rite, every prayer is an incontrovertible witness to *idolatry*. That is why mystical sects of all religions agree in doing away with all rites.

5

Old and New Testament. The basic character of Judaism is *realism* and *optimism*, which are closely related and the preconditions of actual *theism*, since they consider the material world absolutely real and life as a pleasing gift made expressly for us. The basic character of Brahmanism and Buddhism, on the contrary, is *idealism* and *pessimism*, since they allow the world only a dream-like existence and regard life as the consequence of our sins. In the doctrine of the Zend-Avesta [Zoroastrianism], from which Judaism is known to have derived, the pessimistic element is still present and represented by Ahriman. In Judaism, however, he is accorded only a subordinate position as Satan, who is nonetheless still, like Ahriman, the author of snakes, scorpions and vermin. Judaism employs him straightway to repair its fundamental error of optimism, namely to produce the Fall, which then introduces into that religion the pessimistic element required for the sake of fidelity to the most obvious of truths. This element is the most correct basic idea in the religion, although it transfers to the course of existence what ought to be represented as its ground and as preceding it.

The New Testament must be of Indian origin: witness of that is its altogether Indian ethic, in which morality leads to asceticism, its pessimism and its avatar. But it is for precisely this reason that it stands in decided intrinsic opposition to the Old Testament, so that the only thing in the Old Testament which could provide a connecting link with it was the story of the Fall. For when this Indian doctrine entered into the Promised Land there arose the task of uniting the knowledge of the corruption and misery of the world, of its need for redemption and of salvation through an avatar, together with the morality of self-denial and atonement, with Jewish monotheism and its 'Behold, it was very good'. And this union was achieved, as far as it could be; as far, that is, as two so completely heterogeneous, indeed antithetical doctrines *can* be united.

The Creator from nothing, separate from the world, is identified with the Saviour and through him with mankind, whose representative he is, since mankind is redeemed in him as it once fell in Adam and has since lain enmeshed in sin, corruption, suffering and death. For this is how the world appears here as much as it does in Buddhism – and no longer in the light of the Jewish optimism which had found everything 'very good': the Devil himself is now styled 'Prince of this world' (John xii 31). The world is no longer an end, but a means: the kingdom of joy lies beyond it and beyond death. Renunciation in this world and the direction of all hope towards a better world constitutes the spirit of Christianity. The way to such a better world is, however, opened by reconciliation, i.e. redemption from the world and its ways. In morality, the *lex talionis* is replaced by the command to love one's enemy, the promise of a numberless posterity by the promise of eternal life, and the punishment of transgressions to the fourth generation by the Holy Ghost, beneath whose wings everything reposes.

Thus we see the doctrine of the Old Testament rectified and given a new meaning by that of the New, whereby it is made intrinsically and essentially to accord with the ancient religions of India. Everything true in Christianity is also to be discovered in Brahmanism and Buddhism. But the Jewish notion of an animated nothingness, a temporal product which can never be too humbly thankful for an ephemeral existence full of misery, fear and want, nor praise Jehovah too highly for it – this you will look for in vain in Hinduism and Buddhism.

If one wanted to venture on conjectures as to how this agreement with Indian doctrines came about, one might suggest that the Flight into Egypt may rest on some historical fact, and that Jesus was brought up by Egyptian priests, whose religion was of Indian origin, received Indian ethics and the concept of the avatar from them, and afterwards sought to adapt these doctrines to Jewish dogmas and to graft them on to the ancient tree. The feeling of his own moral and intellectual superiority may then have induced him to regard himself as an avatar and consequently to call himself the Son of Man so as to indicate that he was more than simply a man. It is even possible to think that, with the strength and purity of his will and by virtue of the omnipotence which pertains to will in general as thing in itself which we know from the fact of animal magnetism and other magical effects related to it, he was also able to perform so-called miracles, i.e. operate through the metaphysical influence of the will; in connexion with which the instruction he received from the Egyptian priests would likewise have stood him in good stead. Legend would subsequently have exaggerated the number and miraculousness of these miracles. It is only suppositions of this kind which can to some extent explain how Paul, whose principal epistles at least must be genuine, can seriously represent as God incarnate and as one with the Creator of the world a man who has died so recently that many of his contemporaries are still alive: for seriously meant apotheoses of this sort and magnitude usually require many centuries to come gradually to fruition. On the other hand, this consideration could serve as an argument against the genuineness of the Pauline epistles in general.

That the Gospels we possess rest upon an original or at any rate a fragment from the time of Jesus and from his circle I conclude from the objectionable prophecy of the end of the world and of the Lord's glorious Second Coming in the clouds, which is supposed to be going to take place during the lifetime of some of those present when it is promised. For that this promise remained unfulfilled is an extremely vexatious circumstance which proved a stumbling-block not only in later ages but caused embarrassment already to Peter and Paul. If the Gospels, a hundred or so years later, had been indited without the aid of contemporary documents, one would surely have guarded against introducing prophecies of this kind, the non-fulfilment of which had already been brought to light.

The principle laid down by Strauss that the Gospel story, or at any rate its individual detail, is to be explained mythologically is certainly correct, and it will be hard to determine how far this principle extends. As to the nature of myths in general, it will be best to employ less delicate examples closer to hand. Thus, e.g., King Arthur was throughout the Middle Ages, in France as well as in England, a quite authentic person, known for many deeds and always appearing with the same character and the same entourage: with his Round Table, his knights, his heroic acts, his magician, his faithless wife and her Lancelot du Lac, etc., he constituted the standing theme of poets and romancers of many centuries, who all present us with the same characters and agree fairly well in the events they describe, and noticeably differ from one another only in costumes and customs, that is to say according to which age they belong to. Now a few years ago the French government sent M. de la Villemarqué to England to investigate the origin of these myths of King Arthur. The facts behind the myths turned out to be that a petty chieftain named Arthur lived in Wales at the beginning of the sixth century: he fought indefatigably against the invading Saxons, but his insignificant deeds have been forgotten. It is he, then, who, Heaven knows why, became the splendid personage celebrated for many centuries in countless songs, romances and stories. The case is almost the same with Roland, who is the hero of the whole Middle Ages, celebrated in countless songs, epic poems and romances, and even statues, until he was at last transfigured by Ariosto. History, however, refers to him only once, and that only incidentally and in four words: Eginhard includes him in the list of those who stayed behind at Roncesvalles as *Hroudlandus, Britannici limitis praefectus* – and that is all we know about him; just as all we really know about Jesus Christ is the passage in Tacitus.

6

Sects. Augustinianism, with its dogma of original sin and what is associated with it, is, as has already been said, actual Christianity. Pelagianism, on the other hand, is the attempt to take Christianity back to crude and shallow Judaism and its optimism.

The antithesis between Augustinianism and Pelagianism has continually divided the Church: going down to their ultimate ground, one could say that the former speaks of the essence in itself of things, the latter of phenomena which it takes for essence. The Pelagian, e.g., denies original sin, since the child which has as yet done nothing whatever must be innocent: he does this because he does not see that, while the child is a beginning as phenomenon, it is not a beginning as thing in itself. The same consideration applies to free will, to the Saviour's propitiatory death, to grace, in short to everything. – In consequence of its comprehensibility and shallowness, Pelagianism always predominates, but it does so more than ever now, as Rationalism. The Greek Orthodox Church preaches a qualified Pelagianism, as, since the Council of Trent, does the Catholic Church, its object being to set itself in opposition to the Augustinian and consequently mystically minded Luther, and to Calvin: the Jesuits are no less semi-Pelagian. On the other hand, the Jansenists are Augustinian and their doctrine may well be the most genuine form of Christianity. For, by rejecting celibacy and asceticism in general, together with the saints, who are the representatives of asceticism, Protestantism has become a truncated, or rather decapitated Christianity whose apex is missing.

Rationalism. The fundamental distinction between religions does not lie in whether they are monotheistic, polytheistic, pantheistic or atheistic (as Buddhism is), but in whether they are optimistic or pessimistic. The Old and the New Testaments are for this reason diametrically opposed, and their union forms a very strange centaur: for the Old Testament is optimistic, the New Testament pessimistic. The former is a tune in the major, the latter a tune in the minor.

This basic character of Christianity, which Augustine, Luther and Melanchthon perceived very truly and as far as possible systematized, our present-day Rationalists seek to expunge and exegesize away, so as to lead Christianity back to a prosaic, egoistic, optimistic Judaism, adding to it an improved morality and the future life demanded by a consistent optimism, so that the glorious time we are having shall not come to so early an end, and death, which cries out all too loudly against the optimistic outlook and comes at last like the stone guest to the feasting Don Juan, shall be done away with. – These Rationalists are honest but shallow people with no presentiment of the profound meaning of the New Testament myth, who cannot get beyond the optimism of Judaism. They want the plain, unvarnished truth in the domain of history as in that of dogma. They can be compared with the Euhemerists of antiquity. What the supranaturalists bring us is, to be sure, fundamentally a mythology: but this mythology is the vehicle of important

profound truths which cannot be conveyed to the understanding of the great masses in any other way. The
common error of both parties is that they seek in religion
the plain, unvarnished, literal truth. But the plain, unvarnished, literal truth is striven for only in philosophy:
religion possesses only a truth suitable to the people, an
indirect, a symbolic, allegorical truth. Christianity is an
allegory reflecting a true idea; but the allegory itself is
not what is true. To take the allegory for the truth is the
error which supranaturalists and Rationalists agree in
making. The former will assert that the allegory is in
itself true; the latter will twist and bend its meaning until
they have, according to their own lights, made it true in
itself. Each party is accordingly able to make pertinent
and valid points against the other. The Rationalists say
to the supranaturalists: 'Your doctrine isn't true.' The
latter retort: 'Your doctrine isn't Christianity.' Both are
right. The Rationalists believe they are taking reason as
their standard: in fact, however, their standard is only
reason caught up in the presuppositions of theism and
optimism, rather like Rousseau's *Profession de foi du vicaire
savoyard*, that prototype of all Rationalism. Of Christian
dogma they will grant validity to nothing but what
they hold true *sensu proprio*: namely, theism and the
immortality of the soul. While supranaturalism possesses
at any rate allegorical truth, Rationalism cannot be
accorded any truth at all. The Rationalists are simply
wrong. If you would be a Rationalist you will have to be
a philosopher and as such emancipate yourself from
all authority, stride forward and shrink at nothing. If,
however, you would be a theologian you ought to be

consistent and cleave to authority, even if it insists on your believing what is incomprehensible. A man cannot serve two masters: so it is either reason or the scriptures. The *juste milieu* here means falling between two stools. Either believe or philosophize! – whichever you choose, choose wholeheartedly. But to believe up to a certain point and no farther, and to philosophize up to a certain point and no farther – this is the halfheartedness which constitutes the fundamental trait of Rationalism.

Those who think the sciences can go on advancing and spreading wider and wider without threatening the continued existence and prosperity of religion are very much in error. Physics and metaphysics are the natural enemies of religion. To speak of peace and accord between them is very ludicrous: it is a *bellum ad internecionem* [war of extermination]. Religions are the children of ignorance, and they do not long survive their mother. Omar understood that when he burned the library at Alexandria: his reason for doing so – that the knowledge contained in the books was either also contained in the Koran or was superfluous – is regarded as absurd, but is in fact very shrewd if taken *cum grano salis*: it signifies that if the sciences go beyond the Koran they are enemies of religion and consequently not to be tolerated. Christianity would be in much better shape today if Christian rulers had been as wise as Omar. By now, however, it is a little late to burn all the books.

Mankind is growing out of religion as out of its childhood clothes. Faith and knowledge do not get on well together in the same head: they are like a wolf and a sheep in the same cage – and knowledge is the wolf which threatens to eat up its companion. – In its death throes, we see religion clinging to morality, whose mother it would like to pretend to be. In vain! – genuine morality is dependent on no religion, although religion sanctions and thereby sustains it.

Belief is like love: it cannot be compelled; and as any attempt to compel love produces hate, so it is the attempt to compel belief which first produces real unbelief.

8

The reason civilization is at its highest point among *Christian* peoples is not that Christianity is favourable to it but that Christianity is dead and no longer exercises much influence: as long as it did exercise influence, civilization was at a very low point among Christian peoples. All *religion* is antagonistic towards culture.

What a bad conscience religion must have is to be judged by the fact that it is forbidden under pain of such severe punishment to *mock* it.

On Various Subjects

My chief objection to pantheism is that it signifies nothing. To call the world God is not to explain it but merely to enrich the language with a superfluous synonym for the word world. It comes to the same thing whether you say 'the world is God' or 'the world is the world'. If you started from God as that which is given and to be explained, and said 'God is the world', then, to be sure, you would be offering some kind of explanation, inasmuch as it would trace *ignotus* back to *notius*, but still no more than an explanation of a word. But if you start from what actually is given, the world, and say 'the world is God', then it is as plain as day that this says nothing, or at the most explains *ignotum per ignotius*.

It follows that pantheism presupposes the pre-existence of theism: for only by starting from a God, that is to say by already having one and being familiar with him, can you finally come to identify him with the world, actually in order politely to set him aside. You do not start, unprejudiced, from the world as that which is to be explained, you start from God as that which is given, but, soon not knowing what to do with him, you let the world take over his role. That is the origin of pantheism. For it would never occur to anyone taking an unprejudiced view of the world to regard it as a God. It would clearly have to be a very ill-advised God who knew of nothing better to do than to transform himself into a world such as this one.

The great advance which pantheism is supposed to represent over theism is, if taken seriously and not as a mere disguised negation, a transition from the unproved and hardly conceivable to the downright absurd. For however obscure, vague and confused the concept may be which is attached to the word God, two predicates are nonetheless inseparable from it: supreme power and supreme wisdom. But that a being equipped with these should have transplanted himself into a situation such as this world represents is frankly an absurd idea: for our situation in the world is obviously one into which no intelligent, not to speak of all-wise being would transplant himself.

3

A

In the first broad outlines of the Greek system of gods one can glimpse an allegorical representation of the highest ontological and cosmological principles. – Uranus is *space*, the first condition for all existence, thus the first begetter. Cronus is *time*. He castrates the procreative principle: time annihilates all generative power; or more precisely: the capacity for generating *new forms*, the primary generation of living races, ends after the first world-period. Zeus, who is rescued from the voraciousness of his father, is *matter*: it alone escapes the power of time, which destroys everything else: it persists. From matter, however, all other things proceed: Zeus is the father of gods and men.

B

The continuity, indeed the unity of human with animal and all other nature, thus that of the microcosmos with the macrocosmos, is expressed by the mysterious, enigmatic Sphinx, by the centaurs, by Ephesian Artemis with diverse animal forms disposed beneath her countless breasts, as it is by the Egyptian human bodies with animal heads and the Indian Gawesa, and finally by the Ninevite bulls and lions with human heads, which recall the avatar as man-lion.

C

The sons of Iapetus represent four basic qualities of the human character, together with the suffering which comes with them. *Atlas*, the patient, has to bear and endure. *Menoetius*, the brave, is overpowered and hurled to destruction. *Prometheus*, the wise and prudent, is bound, i.e. his effectiveness is limited and a vulture, i.e. care, gnaws at his heart. *Epimetheus*, the rash and thoughtless, is punished by his own folly.

D

I have always found the legend of *Pandora* incomprehensible, indeed preposterous and absurd. I suspect that

Hesiod himself already misunderstood it and distorted its meaning. It is not all the evil but all the good things of the world which Pandora had in her box (as her name already indicates). When Epimetheus rashly opened it the good things flew out and away: Hope alone was saved and still remains with us.

E

It is not without meaning that mythology depicts Cronus as devouring and digesting stones: for that which is otherwise quite indigestible, all affliction, vexation, loss, grief, time alone digests.

F

The downfall of the Titans, whom Zeus hurls into the underworld, seems to be the same story as the downfall of the angels who rebelled against Jehovah.

The story of Idomeneus, who sacrificed his son *ex voto*, and that of Jephtha is essentially the same.

Can it be that, as the root of the Gothic and the Greek languages lies in Sanskrit, so there is an older mythology from which the Greek and the Jewish mythologies derive? If you cared to give scope to your imagination you could even adduce that the twofold-long night in which Zeus begot Heracles on Alcmene came about because further east Joshua at Jericho told the sun to stand still. Zeus and Jehovah were thus assisting one another: for the gods of Heaven are, like those of earth, always secretly in alliance. But how innocent was the pastime of Father Zeus compared with the bloodthirsty activities of Jehovah and his chosen brigands.

G

Viewed from the summit of my philosophy, which, as is well known, is the standpoint of asceticism, the *affirmation of the will to live* is concentrated in the act of procreation and this is its most resolute expression. Now the meaning of this affirmation is intrinsically this, that the will, which is originally without knowledge and thus a blind impulse, arrives at knowledge of its own nature through the world as idea but does not allow itself to be distracted or checked in its desire and passion by this knowledge; it henceforth desires consciously and with full awareness that which it formerly desired as a knowledgeless drive and impulse. In accordance with this, we find that he who ascetically *denies* life through voluntary chastity differs empirically from him who affirms life through acts of procreation in that what takes place without knowledge as a blind physiological function, namely in sleep, in the case of the former, in the case of the latter is carried out with conscious awareness, and thus takes place in the light of knowledge. Now it is in fact very remarkable that this abstract philosophical dictum, which is by no means allied to the spirit of the Greeks, should, together with the empirical events which confirm it, possess an exact allegorical representation in the beautiful legend of *Psyche*, who was permitted to enjoy Amor only if she did not see him but who, ignoring every warning, nonetheless insisted on seeing him, whereupon, in accordance with the ineluctable decree of mysterious powers, she was plunged into limitless misery, which she could emerge from only after a sojourn in the underworld and the performance of heavy tasks there.

5

A

To estimate a *genius* you should not take the mistakes in his productions, or his weaker works, but only those works in which he excels. For even in the realm of the intellect, weakness and absurdity cleave so firmly to human nature that even the most brilliant mind is not always entirely free of them: whence the mighty errors which can be pointed to even in the works of the greatest men, and hence Horace's *Quandoque bonus dormitat Homerus*. What distinguishes genius, on the other hand, and provides a measure for estimating it, is the height to which it was able to rise when time and mood were propitious and which remains for ever unachievable to ordinary talents.

B

The great misfortune for intellectual merit is that it has to wait until the good is praised by those who produce only the bad; indeed, the misfortune already lies in the general fact that it has to receive its crown from the hands of human judgement, a quality of which most people possess about as much as a castrate possesses of the power to beget children.

Power of discrimination, *esprit de discernement*, and consequently judgement: that is what is lacking. They do not know how to distinguish the genuine from the spurious, the wheat from the chaff, gold from tin, and they do not perceive the great distance which separates the commonplace herd from the very rarest. The result is the state of things expressed by the ancient couplet:

> *Es ist nun das Geschick der Grossen hier auf Erden,*
> *Erst wann sie nicht mehr sind, von uns erkannt zu werden.*
> [It is the fate of the great here on earth to be
> recognized by us only when they are no more.]

This lamentable lack of the power to discriminate is no less evident in the sciences, namely in the tenacious life of false and refuted theories. Once come into general credit, they continue to defy truth for centuries. After a hundred years Copernicus had not yet supplanted Ptolemy. Bacon, Descartes, Locke prevailed very slowly and very late. It was no different with Newton: you have only to see the animosity and mockery with which Leibniz opposed the Newtonian gravitational system in his controversy with Clarke. Although Newton lived for almost forty years after the appearance of his *Principia*, his theory was, when he died, recognized only in England, and there only partially, while abroad he could, according to the preface to Voltaire's account of his theory, count fewer than twenty adherents. On the other hand, in our own day Newton's absurd theory of colours still holds the field, forty years after the appearance of Goethe's. Hume, although he started publishing very early and wrote in a thoroughly popular style, was disregarded until his fiftieth year. Kant, although he wrote and taught his whole life long, became famous only after his sixtieth year. – Artists and poets have a better chance than thinkers, to be sure, because their public is at least a hundred times bigger: and yet what did Mozart and Beethoven count for during their lifetime? or Dante, or even Shakespeare? If the contemporaries of this last had had any idea of his worth, that blossoming time of painting would have given us at any rate *one* good, well-attested portrait of him, whereas all we have are a number of altogether doubtful paintings, a very bad engraving and an even worse funeral monument bust. We would likewise possess hundreds of his manuscripts instead of merely a couple of legal signatures. – Every Portuguese is proud of Camoens, the only Portuguese poet: but he lived on alms procured for him in the streets every evening by a Negro boy he had brought back from India.

C

As the sun needs an eye in order to shine, and music an ear in order to sound, so the worth of every masterpiece in art and science is conditioned by the mind related and equal to it to which it speaks. Only such a mind possesses the incantation to arouse the spirits imprisoned in such a work and make them show themselves. The commonplace head stands before it as before a magic casket he cannot open, or before an instrument he cannot play and from which he can therefore summon only inchoate noises, however much he would like to deceive himself in the matter. A beautiful work requires a sensitive mind, a speculative work a thinking mind, in order really to exist and to live.

D

Great minds are related to the brief span of time during which they live as great buildings are to a little square in which they stand: you cannot see them in all their magnitude because you are standing too close to them.

6

A

When you see the many and manifold institutions for teaching and learning and the great crowd of pupils and masters which throngs them you might think the human race was much occupied with wisdom and insight. But here too appearance is deceptive. The latter teach to earn money, and strive not for wisdom but for the appearance of it and to be credited with it; the former learn, not to achieve knowledge and insight, but so as to be able to chatter about them and give themselves airs. Every thirty years a new generation appears which knows nothing and then sets about trying to gulp down summarily and as fast as possible all the human knowledge assembled over the millennia, after which it would like to think it knows more than all the past put together. To this end it resorts to universities and reaches out for books, and for the most recent ones too, as being its own contemporaries and fellows of its own age. Everything quick and everything new! as new as it itself is. And then off it goes, loud with its own opinions!

B

Students and learned men of every kind and every age go as a rule in search of *information*, not *insight*. They make it a point of honour to have information about everything: it does not occur to them that information is merely a *means* towards insight and possesses little or no value in itself. When I see how much these well-informed people know, I sometimes say to myself: Oh, how little such a one must have had to think about, since he has had so much time for reading!

C

The completest erudition compares with genius as a herbarium compares with the ever self-renewing, ever fresh, ever youthful, ever changing plant-world, and there is no greater contrast than that between the erudition of the commentator and the childlike *naïveté* of the ancient author.

D

Dilettantes! Dilettantes! – this is the derogatory cry those who apply themselves to art or science for the sake of gain raise against those who pursue it for love of it and pleasure in it. This derogation rests on their vulgar conviction that no one would take up a thing seriously unless prompted to it by want, hunger, or some other kind of greediness. The public has the same outlook and consequently holds the same opinion, which is the origin of its universal respect for 'the professional' and its mistrust of the dilettante. The truth, however, is that to the dilettante the thing is the end, while to the professional as such it is the means; and only he who is directly interested in a thing, and occupies himself with it from love of it, will pursue it with entire seriousness. It is from such as these, and not from wage-earners, that the greatest things have always come.

7

A

In accordance with the nature of our intellect, *concepts* ought to arise through abstraction from our *perceptions*, consequently perception should precede concept. If this has in fact happened, as it has in the case of the man whose own experience is his only book and teacher, then he knows quite well what perceptions belong to which of his concepts and are represented by them. We may call this 'natural education'.

In the case of artificial education, on the contrary, the head is, through lectures, teaching and reading, stuffed full of concepts before there is any wide acquaintanceship with the perceptual world at all. Experience is then supposed to supply the perceptions to fit these concepts: up to that time, however, they have been wrongly applied, and things and men consequently wrongly judged, wrongly seen, wrongly dealt with. So it happens that education produces wrong-headedness, and that is why in youth, after much reading and learning, we go out into the world in part naïve, in part confused, and conduct ourselves in it now with arrogance, now with timidity: our heads are full of concepts which we are now endeavouring to apply, but which we almost always apply wrongly.

B

In accordance with the foregoing, the chief factor in education would be that *acquaintanceship with the world*, the achievement of which we may designate the object of all education, should *begin from the right end*. This, however, depends, as has been shown, on *perception* always preceding *concept*, and further on the narrower concept preceding the wider, and the entire course of instruction thus proceeding in the order in which concepts *presuppose* one another. As soon, however, as something in this series is overleaped, there arise defective concepts, and from these false concepts, and finally a wrong-headed view of the world, of which almost everyone carries his own version around in his head, some for a long time, most for ever. Correct understanding of many quite simple things comes only when one is advanced in years, and sometimes it then comes suddenly: there has been as it were a blind spot in one's acquaintanceship with the world, originating in an overleaping of the subject in one's early education, whether this education was an artificial one or a natural one through one's own experience.

C

Because errors imbibed early are mostly ineradicable and because the reasoning faculty is the last to mature, children should not, until they are sixteen, be exposed to any subject in which major errors are possible, that is to say philosophy, religion and general views of all kinds; they should be introduced only to those in which error is either impossible, as in mathematics, or of no great moment, as in languages, natural science, history, etc., in general however only to such studies as are accessible to their age and completely comprehensible. Childhood and youth is the time for assembling data and for becoming specifically and thoroughly acquainted with individual things; reasoning and judgement in general must remain in suspense and ultimate explanations be deferred. Since the reasoning faculty presupposes maturity and experience, it should be let alone for the time being: the impression of prejudices upon it before it is mature will damage it for good.

D

Maturity of knowledge, i.e. the degree of perfection to which knowledge can attain in each individual, consists in this, that in every case an exact correspondence has been achieved between abstract concept and perceptual comprehension, so that every concept rests directly or indirectly on a perceptual basis, through which alone it possesses real value, and that every perception can likewise be subsumed under the concept appropriate to it. Maturity is solely the work of experience and consequently of time. For, since we usually acquire our perceptual and our abstract knowledge separately, the former by natural means, the latter through good or bad instruction and communication from others, there is in youth usually little correspondence between our concepts, which have been fixed by mere words, and the real knowledge we have acquired through perception. These approach one another only gradually and mutually correct one another: but only when they are entirely united is our knowledge mature.

8

The animal voice serves only to express excitement and agitation of the *will*; the human, however, serves also to express *knowledge*; this is consistent with the fact that the former almost always makes an unpleasant impression on us, the voices of a few birds alone excepted.

When human language began to evolve, the beginning was certainly made by *interjections*, which express not concepts but, like the sounds made by animals, feelings, agitations of the will. The differences between them soon made themselves felt, and out of this difference there arose the transition to substantives, verbs, personal pronouns, etc.

The word of man is the most durable of all material. Once a poet has embodied his fleeting sensations in words appropriate to them, they live on in those words through the millennia and stir anew in every receptive reader.

9

That the outer mirrors the inner, and that the countenance expresses and reveals the whole essence of a man, is a presupposition whose a-priority and consequent certainty is manifested in the universal desire to *see* any man who has made himself prominent in any way, whether for good deeds or bad, or who has produced some extraordinary work; or, if this proves impossible, to learn from others *what he looks like*. Likewise, in everyday life, everyone inspects the face of anyone he meets and silently tries to discover in advance from his physiognomy his moral and intellectual nature. None of this would be so if, as some fools believe, a man's appearance possessed no significance and the body bore no closer relation to the soul than the coat does to the body.

The contrary is the case: every human face is a hieroglyph which can be deciphered, indeed whose key we bear ready-made within us. It is even true that a man's face as a rule says more, and more interesting things than his mouth, for it is a compendium of everything his mouth will ever say, in that it is the monogram of all this man's thoughts and aspirations. The mouth, further, expresses only the thoughts of a man, while the face expresses a thought of nature: so that everyone is worth looking at, even if everyone is not worth talking to.

We all proceed on the basis of the unspoken rule that every man *is* as he *looks*: this is a correct rule; the difficulty lies in applying it. The capacity for doing so is in part inborn, in part to be gained through experience, but no one ever perfects it: even the most practised detect errors in themselves. Yet the face does not lie: it is we who read what is not written there. In any event, the deciphering of the face is a great and difficult art. Its principles can never be learned *in abstracto*. The first precondition for practising it is that you must take a *purely objective* view of your man, which is not so easy to do: for as soon as the slightest trace of aversion, or partiality, or fear, or hope, or even the thought of what impression we ourselves are making on *him*, in short as soon as anything subjective is involved, the hieroglyph becomes confused and corrupted. Just as we can hear the sound of a language only if we do not understand it, because otherwise what is signified at once suppresses consciousness of the sign which signifies it, so we can see the physiognomy of a man only if he is a stranger to us: consequently one can, strictly speaking, receive a purely objective impression of a face, and thus have the possibility of deciphering it, only at first sight.

Let us not dissemble over the fact that this first sight is usually extremely disagreeable. With the exception of the beautiful, good-natured or intelligent faces – with the exception, that is, of a very few, rare faces – I believe that every new face will usually arouse in a person of finer feeling a sensation akin to terror, since it presents the disagreeable in a new and surprising combination. As a rule it is in truth a sorry sight. There are even some upon whose face there is imprinted such naïve vulgarity and lowness of character combined with such beast-like narrowness of mind that one wonders why they go around with such a face and do not rather wear a mask. Indeed, there are faces at the mere sight of which one feels polluted. – The *metaphysical* explanation of this fact would involve the consideration that the individuality of each man is precisely that of which, through his existence itself, he is to be cured. If, on the other hand, you are content with the *psychological* explanation, you should ask yourself what kind of physiognomy is to be expected of those in whom in the course of a long life there has very rarely arisen anything but petty, base, miserable thoughts and common, selfish, base and mischievous desires. Each of them, while it was present, set its mark on his face, and by much repetition deeply engraved itself there.

11

D

A mother had, for their education and betterment, given her children Aesop's fables to read. Very soon, however, they brought the book back to her, and the eldest, who was very knowing and precocious, said: 'This is not a book for us! It's much too childish and silly. We've got past believing that foxes, wolves and ravens can talk: we're far too grown-up for such nonsense!' – Who cannot see in this hopeful lad the future enlightened Rationalist?

THE STORY OF PENGUIN CLASSICS

Before 1946 ... 'Classics' are mainly the domain of academics and students, without readable editions for everyone else. This all changes when a little-known classicist, E. V. Rieu, presents Penguin founder Allen Lane with the translation of Homer's Odyssey that he has been working on and reading to his wife Nelly in his spare time.

1946 The Odyssey becomes the first Penguin Classic published, and promptly sells three million copies. Suddenly, classic books are no longer for the privileged few.

1950s Rieu, now series editor, turns to professional writers for the best modern, readable translations, including Dorothy L. Sayers's *Inferno* and Robert Graves's *The Twelve Caesars*, which revives the salacious original.

1960s 1961 sees the arrival of the Penguin Modern Classics, showcasing the best twentieth-century writers from around the world. Rieu retires in 1964, hailing the Penguin Classics list as 'the greatest educative force of the 20th century'.

1970s A new generation of translators arrives to swell the Penguin Classics ranks, and the list grows to encompass more philosophy, religion, science, history and politics.

1980s The Penguin American Library joins the Classics stable, with titles such as *The Last of the Mohicans* safeguarded. Penguin Classics now offers the most comprehensive library of world literature available.

1990s Penguin Popular Classics are launched, offering readers budget editions of the greatest works of literature. Penguin Audiobooks brings the classics to a listening audience for the first time, and in 1999 the launch of the Penguin Classics website takes them online to an ever larger global readership.

The 21st Century Penguin Classics are rejacketed for the first time in nearly twenty years. This world famous series now consists of more than 1,300 titles, making the widest range of the best books ever written available to millions – and constantly redefining the meaning of what makes a 'classic'.

The Odyssey continues ...

The best books ever written

PENGUIN ⬤ CLASSICS

SINCE 1946

Find out more at www.penguinclassics.com